LINGUISTICS, PHONICS,
and the
TEACHING OF READING

LINGUISTICS, PHONICS,
and the
TEACHING OF READING

By

EMERALD DECHANT

Professor of Education
Fort Hays Kansas State College
Hays, Kansas

CHARLES C THOMAS · PUBLISHER
Springfield · Illinois · U.S.A.

Published and Distributed Throughout the World by
CHARLES C THOMAS · PUBLISHER
Bannerstone House
301-327 East Lawrence Avenue, Springfield, Illinois, U.S.A.
Natchez Plantation House
735 North Atlantic Boulevard, Fort Lauderdale, Florida, U.S.A.

With THOMAS BOOKS *careful attention is given to all details of
manufacturing and design. It is the Publisher's desire to present books
that are satisfactory as to their physical qualities and artistic possibilities
and appropriate for their particular use.* THOMAS BOOKS *will be true
to those laws of quality that assure a good name and good will.*

Printed in the United States of America
B-7

*To my wife, Deloris,
and to our children,
Randy, Lori, Pami*

PREFACE

Rᴇsᴇᴀʀᴄʜ and observation point to one basic fact: the child needs to learn a "coding system" which permits him to attack new words with ease and with accuracy. In 1964, in our book *Improving the Teaching of Reading*[19] we wrote:

> In reading, good teaching seems to mean that the teacher must devise techniques of instruction which help the pupil to construct a generic code or a coding system that has wider applicability in reading than would the rote identification of individual words. The code has wider application than in the situation in which it was learned. The child learns to "read off" from this generic code information that permits him to attack other words . . . . The child, in a sense, must be taught to be a better guesser by knowing the language system and the phonogram-phoneme interrelationships.

The system of linguistic phonics which we develop in this book provides the pupil with such a system. However, this system cannot be taught to pupils unless the teacher knows it. This is then the purpose of this small book.

The book is designed to provide teachers with the principles and the knowledge necessary to help the pupil develop a coding system of his own. In each instance, principles are accompanied by actual application. Teachers must know *what* phonic skills need to be taught, *when* to teach them, *why* they should be taught, and *how* they should be taught.

Recent studies indicate that teachers as a group have not attained the phonic sophistication that they might.

A study by Aaron,[1] involving 293 students enrolled in an introductory reading course, suggests that many teachers and prospective teachers need to acquire in college even the most basic phonic generalizations—213 students (73%) got fewer than forty items of a sixty-item phonics test correct. The mean score of correct answers was 34. The composition of the group was as follows: 189 without teaching experience; 42 with one to five years of experience; 24 with six to ten years; and 38 with ten or more years experience. Teachers with experience generally scored better than those without experience, but teachers at the primary level did not score better than teachers at other grade levels. Spache and Baggett's[50] study essentially corroborated these findings, but their experienced teachers had no greater knowledge of syllabication principles than did the inexperienced teachers. The teachers answered correctly 75 per cent of the questions on phonics, 91 per cent of the ones on syllabication, and 68 per cent of the ones on syllabication rules. The teachers in junior and senior high schools were significantly poorer in knowledge of phonics.

The items on Aaron's test measured ability in dealing with the following:

1. Vowels in open syllables.
2. Vowels in closed syllables.
3. Silent *e* preceded by a long vowel (mete).
4. Long vowel before a silent second vowel (boat).
5. *C* before *e*, *i*, or *y*.
6. *G* before *e*, *i*, or *y*.
7. Vowels followed by *r*.
8. The vowel *a* followed by *l*.

Ramsey,[47] after studying reading manuals to determine what phonic skills the teacher of reading needed, developed a test to measure the teacher's competencies in these. He then administered the *Test of Word Recognition Skills* to 236 students from five teacher-education colleges. All of the students were planning to become elementary teachers and had not yet taken the first course in methods of teaching reading.

The students knew their consonant sounds, but were weak in vowels, in the differences between short and long vowels, in diphthongs, and in verbalizing principles or rules governing phonic and letter relationships.

Austin and her associates[2] also found that many classroom teachers are not adequately prepared to teach the skills required for successful reading.

But even with these seeming weaknesses the reader might ask, Why another book on phonics? The reason is simply that we have not made use of the significant advances in linguistic knowledge in the teaching of phonics. This is the reason we have titled the book *Linguistics, Phonics, and The Teaching of Reading*. Linguistics and phonics need to be combined if each is to be taught well.

We have undertaken the writing of this book with a degree of apprehensiveness. Phonics instruction and knowledge of the characteristics that individualize words present so many elements that the end result might be confusion rather than clarity of insight. If a child had to learn and had to be taught formally every contrast as an individual unit of knowledge or indeed even if he had to learn formally every principle or generalization proposed in the book before he learned to read, few might be termed readers and those of us who are readers would gladly exclaim, "Thank God, I have learned to read."

Yet, the good reader has a functional knowledge of the phonic skills discussed in the book.

It would seem also that the artful teacher needs a much vaster, more systematic, and more generalized knowledge than the good reader. He needs to know *why* a word is pronounced as it is. He needs to be familiar with the complexities of our language.

The various sections of this book can be used as references when the teacher needs to teach specific phonic skills in the classroom. This does not tie the teacher to the sequence suggested in this volume. In each instance we have presented common monosyllabic words that best illustrate the sound that is being considered.

The teacher should remember that phonic skill is not developed overnight. It is impossible to suggest at what time children should have mastered the phonic skills or indeed whether they ever need to master all of them. Not every child can learn every skill. There will be and should be individual differences in this area as in most other areas of human accomplishment.

To accomplish our goals we have divided the book into the following chapters:

CONTENTS

LINGUISTICS, PHONICS,
and the
TEACHING OF READING

I
INTRODUCTION TO LINGUISTIC PHONICS

O ᴠᴇʀ the years much debate has centered about the question, Should the teaching of reading begin with an analytic approach or the whole word or with a synthetic approach or a part of the word?

In Chapter 8 of our book *Improving the Teaching of Reading*[19] we outlined the pros and cons of this question and reached certain conclusions. Let us summarize these here.

1. The mode of identifying a word initially is different from recognizing the word after it has been learned. The appropriate method of recognizing a word may not be the appropriate method of teaching word identification. Even though the mature reader may react to the total word in recognition and meaningful interpretation, it does not follow that he does so in learning to identify the word. The unit of meaning and of recognition may not be the unit of identification. Or to put it another way, words may be the basic meaning units but are not necessarily the basic units of visual identification or even of recognition.

2. The letter is as much a gestalt or total form as is the word. The word form or its configuration is not any more meaningful than is a single letter. The word form becomes meaningful to the learner only if he can see the interrelationships of its parts. To say that a word form is *meaningful* is not the same as saying that it has *meaning*.

3. Mature readers are capable of perceiving more complex gestalten than are beginning readers, but even they have to analyze some words into their parts.

4. The perceptual whole is a relative term. It is not the same for all children in all circumstances. There is no evidence to indicate how much the so-called unit entails. It may be a sentence or a letter. Just as a word is both a *whole* and a *part*, so also a letter is both a *whole* and a *part*.

5. It is rather arbitrary to say that for every child the perceptual whole is the word. Surely, what constitutes the whole is dependent upon the ability, experience, purposes, maturation, perceptual skill, and learning habits of the learner. It also depends on the nature of the materials being learned. The psychology of individual differences suggests that each child characteristically reacts to the *perceptual whole*, but that for one child it may be the total word, for another, it may be part of a word. In general, the whole child reacts, but he is not necessarily stimulated holistically.

3

Perception is holistic only if the form itself is quite simple and uncomplicated. If the whole is meaningless to the perceiver, the details tend to dominate individual perception. The smallest unit of meaningfulness in perception must necessarily be a whole.

6. Valid reasons for beginning with the whole word are the following:

   a. Any method of reading must keep meaning in the limelight. Reading is never complete without the apprehension of meaning. Reading is the process of securing meaning, and it would seem that from the beginning the child should be dealing with meaningful language units. Thus the child from the beginning should be introduced to the smallest linguistic unit that can stand alone and that has meaning. This is the word. He should learn that he is responding to a symbol with which he can associate meaning—not necessarily systematic meaning but referential meaning. Words have meaning; the sounds of the individual letters in a word do not.

      Starting with the word and meaning makes learning to read an interesting and rewarding process from the beginning. These side effects perhaps have greater significance for successful learning and for the development of habitual reading than the method that is used.

   b. The pupil has had numerous experiences with words, listening to them and speaking them.

   c. There is a one-to-one relationship between the spoken word and the printed word symbol, even though the spelling irregularities are many.

   d. There are, finally, many words that cannot be learned letter by letter or sound by sound. These words often defy phonic analysis and must be learned as sight words.

7. It is not efficient however, for the learner to identify each word as a new squiggle. He needs to be able to identify new words independently and with ease. To accomplish this two things are necessary.

   a. The pupil needs to learn a coding system which permits him to capitalize upon the sound-print relationships, upon the phoneme-phonogram interrelationships of the English language. Word recognition then becomes a process of decoding the unknown printed word through the appreciation of one's knowledge of grapheme-phoneme correspondences.

   b. The teacher needs to be able to organize his presentation of words in such a way that children can break the code.

The program of linguistic phonics which we have outlined in this book is designed to accomplish these ends. It hopes to guide the teacher in helping the pupil to develop a coding system, and it suggests how the program can be organized in the classroom so that the pupil can learn to break the code.

Word-attack skills are needed to attain one of the basic goals of the teaching of reading. It is hoped that the reader eventually will commit the word so well to memory that he can respond to it spontaneously without having "to figure it out." Each word should then become a sight word—a word that is instantly recognized.

Phonetic instruction (and consequently phonetic analysis) is not reading; it is only one of the skills required for successful reading. It is not even the only method of word attack. Other ways of identifying and recognizing a word are through the use of picture clues, the use of the configuration of the word, the use of context clues, and structural analysis. Weber[52] found that children use all types of cues (phonic, grammatical, and meaning) to recognize words, but he also noted that toward the end of first grade, children become more reliant upon phonic cues. The high-achieving children used phonic cues to a greater degree than did the nonachievers.

Phonics is no longer a real issue in reading. All systematized approaches to reading teach phonics in one way or another. All approaches stress the importance of attaining meaning. Thus, all emphasize both analytical and synthetic approaches. However, there are differences as to the route to ultimate progress in reading. Should the earliest emphasis be on meaning or on word discrimination? We believe that this is a pseudoquestion and that both are essential from the beginning. There must be a delicate balance between the two, lest the child be dragged too far afield in either. There must be a middle course between a complete discrimination approach in which pupils perhaps can recognize words but cannot comprehend what they are reading, and a meaning approach in which children might be able to enjoy reading but cannot recognize the words.

In the configuration approach, the printed word is directly associated with an idea; in the word-discrimination approach, greater emphasis is placed on the association of the printed word with the spoken word for which the child has a meaning. The first of these has been an effective way for introducing reading. It seems that the second is essential to develop independence in reading. Children need to see words as units, but they also need to pay attention to parts. We do not want to have children capable of reacting only to the whole, neither do we want them to become fixated on the parts.

The child, in this approach to reading, must be viewed as a learner capable of discrimination and generalization who can, with guidance, learn a generalized coding system which he can use in identifying numerous words not previously seen by him.

Terminology

Before getting into the specifics of linguistic phonics instruction, let us clarify a few terms.

1. *Descriptive linguistics* is the most basic branch of linguistics. It is subdivided into phonology and grammar. Phonology is the study of the sounds of a language. Grammar is composed of morphology (a study of the structure of words) and syntax (a study of the way words are grouped into utterances).

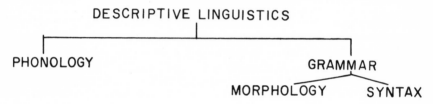

DESCRIPTIVE LINGUISTICS

PHONOLOGY   GRAMMAR

MORPHOLOGY   SYNTAX

Grammar has only one basic function: to make our utterances clearer. It is an aid to the expression and interpretation of meaning. Morphology, for example, allows us to introduce minute changes into the word to bring out a special meaning. The various uses of *s* are examples of this: run*s*, cat*s*. Syntax permits us to group words to suggest certain nuances of meaning. For example, the same words might be grouped in this way to suggest various meanings: "The weak girl is playing a game of tennis," or "The girl is playing a weak game of tennis"; "The boy sat in a chair with a broken arm," or "The boy with a broken arm sat in a chair"; "The lion in the cage roared at the man," or "The lion roared at the man in the cage." Punctuation in writing and pauses in speech are not so much an aid to writing and speaking as they are to reading and listening. The writer knows what the sentences mean; he does not need grammatical aids to get the meaning.

2. *Phonemics* is the study of the speech sounds that are used in language. It is thus a study of phonemes. Phonemic analysis deals only with those sounds that are significant in the language (the phonemes) and ignores the non-significant differences (the allophones). The *p* sound in pet, spot, suppose, and top is slightly different in each instance, but the difference is considered to be nonsignificant. The phonemes are the smallest sound units in a language. Phonemes combine to form morphemes which are the smallest units of language that can bear meaning. The written phoneme is a grapheme, and the writing of graphemes in proper order to form morphemes is orthography or spelling.

The phoneme has one prime purpose in language: it individualizes human utterances. The phoneme is the smallest unit of language which can differentiate one utterance from another. For example, the sentence "Tom, will you wash these carrots?" and "Tom, will you wash those carrots?" are completely alike except for one phoneme. A single letter representing a simple sound changes completely the meaning of the following sentences: "A stitch in time saves none," or "There's no business like shoe business." "The phonological system of language is therefore not so much a 'set of sounds' as it is a network of differences between sounds."[33]*

3. *Phonetics* is the study of the sounds used in speech, including their pronunciations, the symbolization of the sounds, and the action of the larynx, tongue, and lips in sound production. Phonetics does not concern itself with the ways words are spelled by the traditional alphabet. It seeks to develop phonetic alphabets which represent graphically the actual pronunciations of linguistic forms. Dictionaries contain phonetic transliterations.

4. *Phonics* is the study of the speech equivalents of printed symbols and the use of this knowledge in identifying and pronouncing printed words.[30] It is learning which involves the association of the appearance of a letter or letter combinations with a given sound.[30] It is the study of sound-letter relationships in reading and spelling. Phonics instruction represents the various teaching practices that aim to develop the pupil's ability to sound out a word by matching individual letters by which a word is spelled with the specific sounds which these letters say. *Phonic analysis* is the actual process of sounding out letters or letter combinations to arrive at the pronunciation of the word.

5. *The alphabet* is a set of graphic shapes that represent the phonemes of the language.

6. *Word analysis* is an inclusive term which subsumes all methods of attacking words. Phonics is one form of word analysis.

7. *Phonic or phonetic method*, one of various methods of teaching reading, is often considered to be a synthetic method because it begins with the word element or the sound of the letter and gradually advances to the total word. This designation is actually in error. There are some *phonic methods* that are termed *whole-word phonics* which begin with the total word.

8. *A linguist* is a scientist who studies a language in terms of its basic structure, including sound patterns, stress, intonation, and syntactic structure.

9. *Linguistic phonics*—we have titled this chapter "Introduction to Linguistic Phonics" because we recommend that the letter be sounded only in the context of the total word—sometimes is referred to as the phonemic-word approach because the structure of the language is studied through symbol-sound relationships in whole words. It is our view that the method of comparing and contrasting basic spelling patterns with the appropriate or

* From *A Course in Modern Linguistics*, by C. H. Hockett. Copyright © 1958. Reprinted by permission of Macmillan Co.

correlative sound patterns leads to independence in attacking new words. Thus, the individual letter is never sounded; it is only named. The sounds represented by *b, c, d* exist only in the context of a word or syllable. The *o* combination with *y* as in *boy* has a distinct sound; its sound depends on the pattern in which it occurs. Blending, which is a common problem in phonics, ought not to be a problem in a linguistic approach.

Whenever the word *phonics* is used alone in this book, it is meant to signify whole-word phonics as opposed to synthetic phonics.

The Phonetic Consistency of Our Language

A common complaint is that the English language is too inconsistent and that it therefore is impossible to develop a reliable coding system. Certainly, the teaching of reading has paid relatively little attention to the phonic consistency of the English language, even such as it is. And yet, Hanna and Moore[28] found English to be 86.9 per cent phonetic. We do not mean that English is less phonetic than other languages. It is not correct to say that one language is more phonetic than another. All languages, in that they involve the use of phonemes or speech sounds, are phonetic. One language may have a more consistent spelling system and thus is more alphabetic than another. Thus, Hanna and Moore report that single consonants are represented by regular spellings about 90 per cent of the time.

Ever so often in the literature somebody pokes fun at anyone who talks of phonic consistency. It also is not difficult to find examples of the difficulties that one would encounter if one assumed that the English language provided a completely consistent spelling system for the sounds of the language. Systems like ITA and Words in Color were developed precisely because there are so many inconsistencies. George Bernard Shaw asserted, years ago, that the word *fish* might just as well be spelled *ghoti*. There is no doubt that the *f* sound is sometimes spelled *gh* (enough); the short *i* sound, as *o* (women); and the *sh* sound, as *ti* (nation). But, Lefevre[36] notes that not any of the three phonemes is regularly represented in these positions by these graphemes in actual spelling practice. The *gh* is never used initially; *ti* representing *sh* occurs medially or at the initial part of a suffix such as *-tion* or *-tiate*, but never at the end of a word; and *o* occurs as short *i* precisely once in English and that is in the word *women*.

The correspondence between written and spoken English is weak if one attempts to relate individual letters and sounds, but if the graphemic unit is a letter pattern, words, or word groups, a high degree of correspondence is found.[35]

To deal with the irregularities of the language, especially in beginning reading, reading specialists have often severely restricted the vocabulary. However, Levin and Watson's studies[38,39] should be given serious thought before restricting vocabulary too much. They found that training on regular sound-to-spelling correspondences was less than optimal for transfer. Levin suggests that it seems reasonable early in one's schooling to simultaneously learn more than one associated sound to letters and letter groups. The indication is that this will lead to greater flexibility in trying out sounds when the child meets new instances. The study showed that dual associations were more difficult to acquire; but that once acquired, they facilitated the child's learning to read new words.

Linguistic Systems of Teaching Reading

Since we have termed the approach used in this book linguistic phonics, it may be advantageous to summarize various linguistic systems of teaching reading. There is really no linguistic method; all methods of teaching reading are linguistic methods in that they teach the comprehension of linguistic material.

Bloomfield and Barnhart[8,9] presented in 1961 a linguistic approach in *Let's Read: A Linguistic Approach*. They emphasized that reading is primarily a language process and that the major task facing the child is the mastery of the graphic system that reflects the spoken-language system. The central thesis of the Bloomfield-Barnhart method is that there is an inseparable relationship between the words as printed and the sounds for which the letters are conventional signs, and that converting letters to meaning requires from the beginning a concentration upon letter and sound to bring about as rapidly as possible an automatic association between them. Barnhart[9] points out that Bloomfield's system is a linguistic system of teaching reading which separates the problem of the study of word-form from the study of word-meaning. He notes that children come to school knowing how to speak the English language, but they do not know how to read the form of words.

Bloomfield makes the following points:

1. In spite of its many imperfections, the system of writing used in the English language is basically alphabetic, and reading is merely the act of responding vocally to the printed letter as it functions with other letters. The alphabetic nature of our writing is most obvious when we put together a combination of letters to make a word. The linguistic emphasis thus is not so much on the representation of a single phoneme, but rather of a pattern of phonemes. The emphasis is on the relationship between patterns of phonemes and patterns of graphemes, especially between spoken words and written words. The linguist admits that the correspondence between written and spoken English often is weak if one relates individual letters and sounds, but notes that the correspondence between letter patterns and word groups is high. The letter is not sounded alone; it is sounded only in the context of other letters or the word.

2. In order to read alphabetic writing, the reader must have developed an ingrained habit of producing the phonemes of the language when he sees the written marks which conventionally represent these phonemes.

3. English writing is alphabetic, but only imperfectly so. The child should not be introduced to the exceptions until he has mastered the regularities of the language. The child's early reading experiences should be dealing with letters and sounds as they function in monosyllabic regular words. Hildreth[32] notes that it is easier to learn the relationships among sound elements within words by studying monosyllabic words. When all words are three-letter words, the pupil cannot use the length of the word to identify it and quite frequently he cannot use the configuration: *bat, hat.* Both words obviously have the same configuration. The words should contain only short vowels. Long vowel sounds, diphthongs, consonant blends, speech consonants, and words containing silent letters should be introduced only after the pupil has mastered some of the phonetic consistencies of the language. The goal of this approach to reading instruction is to familiarize children with the phonetic consistencies of the language as a basis for generalizations to new words. In beginning reading materials, every letter should represent only one single phoneme. The pupil must learn this equation:

   printed letter = speech sound to be spoken.

   The first material should contain no words with silent letters (*k*nit), none with double letters (be*ll*), and none with combinations of letters having a special value (*ea* as in *bean*). Letters such as *x* or *q* should also be taught later.

4. Bloomfield decries the fact that synthetic phonic methods isolate speech sounds. Synthetic phonics proceeds as though the child were being taught to speak. Phonemes do not occur by themselves and should not be taught in isolation.

5. The child should first be taught the names of the letters. Presenting the

letters in color increases interest and emphasizes shape. Writing of the letters should be delayed until after reading has begun.

Lefevre,[36,37] having a different emphasis from that of Bloomfield, adapted linguistic ideas to meaningful reading. He suggests an analytical method of teaching reading emphasizing language patterns. He emphasized that meaning comes only through the grasping of the language structure exemplified in a sentence. Meaning thus depends on the intonation, the word and sentence order, the grammatical inflections, and certain key-function words. Intonation, or the pauses and stresses in oral language, are represented by (1) capital letters, periods, semicolons, and question marks, (2) by the order of the words, (3) by grammatical inflections signaling tense, number, and possession, and (4) by such function words as *the*, *when*, *nevertheless*, or *because*. Only by reading structures can full meaning be attained. Or, to put it another way, unless the reader translates correctly the printed text into the intonation pattern of the writer, he may not be getting the meaning intended.

Bloomfield felt that initial teaching of reading for meaning is incorrect and that meaning will come quite naturally as the alphabetic code or principle is discovered. Lefevre is critical of Bloomfield's approach, criticizing him for confining himself largely to phonemic analysis and for neglecting intonation and syntax.

Lefevre[36] makes the following observations:

1. To comprehend printed matter, the reader must learn to perceive and to recognize and interpret the graphic counterparts of entire spoken utterances as unitary meaning-bearing patterns. This is reading comprehension.

2. Lefevre decries the emphasis on letters and words as the significant units of language. He notes that in English the most significant structures are intonation pattern, grammatical and syntactical words groups, clauses, and sentences. Words are relatively minor elements in meaning-bearing patterns. The pupil needs to be taught to read by language patterns that carry meaning. Word order provides one of the most reliable clues to the total meaning-bearing pattern. Intonation is another. The child should be taught first to read and write the language patterns he brings to school. Writing and print are phonemic devices whose chief function is to effect recall of entire language patterns, especially sentence-level utterances.

4. Misapprehension of the relationships between spoken and printed language or sentence patterns is a decisive element in reading failures. The basic fault in poor reading is poor sentence sense, often demonstrated

orally in word-calling. The crippled reader's worst fault is literal word-calling or word-by-word reading with virtually no sentence sense. The poor reader registers only random elements (words)—many cannot even do this, and that is why we need phonics—but misses language structures altogether.

5. Children taught to read with chief emphasis on larger patterns than words develop their own generalizations of spelling-sound relationships (phonics). If they do not, special instruction may need to be devised to help them. Although attention to word analysis and spelling may be necessary, isolated words must be brought back into the larger patterns and structures that function linguistically and carry meaning; this is true reading.

Fries[25] offers the following suggestions for the teaching of reading:*

1. The process of learning to read "is the *process of transfer* from the auditory signs for language signals [sounds], which the child has already learned, to the new visual signs [letters} for the same signals."

   Reading and talking have the same set of language signals for language reception. In speech, contrastive bundles of sound features represent these signals; in reading, contrastive patterns of spelling represent the same signals.

2. Writing represents the time sequence of auditory patterns (sounds follow one another in time) by means of sequence of direction in space. In English writing, the space-direction is a horizontal sequence of graphic shapes from left to right.

3. The first set of recognition responses which the pupil must develop are those for the letters of our alphabet. The letters must be identified as contrasting shapes. This does not necessarily mean attaching the conventional names to the letters even though the names are useful in checking the identification response.

4. At this level there should be no attempt to connect the letters themselves with specific sounds, and the groups of letters (such as *it, if, fit, hit, at, hat*) should not be pronounced as words or be connected with meanings.

   The approach advocated by Fries rests upon the same foundation as does phonics, namely, the relation between sound patterns of the words and the letter symbols of the alphabet, but it differs in that the relation is not such as to lead to the matching of specific letters with each of the physical sounds of the language. Reading is not the matching of words, letter by letter, with words, sound by sound. Furthermore, the pronunciation of a word is not a fusion or blending of the sounds represented by the individual letters.

   The pupil must develop the automatic habits of responding to the contrastive features of spelling patterns as identifying the word patterns they represent. For example, even in the three letter word *man* it is not the single letter *a* that indicates the vowel sound *ae*. "It is the spelling pattern *m a n* in contrast with the spelling pattern *m a n e* or that of *m e a n* that signals the different vowel phonemes that make these three different words."

5. This spelling-pattern approach, namely, learning to respond to the contrastive features that identify whole word patterns, is a word method. The basic difference between this spelling-pattern approach and the usual word method lies in the kind of identifying characteristics used to recognize the words. These are the identifying characteristics of the language itself as they are incorporated in the patterns of our alphabetic spelling.

6. "(a) The words used, that is, the sound patterns of the words themselves and the particular meanings selected, must include only those within the *actual linguistic experience* of the pupil. The beginning reading stage must use only the language material already in the full control of the pupil; it is not the time to strive to increase the range of that control.

(b) The grammatical signals must also include only those within the pupil's linguistic experience. By the age of four or five, however, most native speakers of English will have full control of practically all the basic grammatical signals of their language. . . .

(c) Not all the words familiar to the pupil in the transfer stage of reading can be used for the materials of practice. It is essential *throughout this stage* that the words selected for the practice materials be only those for which *the spelling patterns fit those that have been introduced and practiced.* . . .

(d) . . . The simple contrasts used should always be of items within a whole word pattern, never of items less than a word. . . .

(e) . . . Only complete words are pronounced. The pronunciation for the "word" is thus attached to the total spelling pattern that represents that word. The spelling pattern *c a t* represents the word [kaet] as pronounced. . . . The understanding of the difference that any particular letter makes in the spelling pattern is built up out of the experience of pronouncing a variety of word pairs with minimum differences in their *spelling patterns*.

cat—at
cat—rat
cat—pat

We should avoid completely such a question as what does the letter C say?

7. "And yet if the reader is to learn to read well, that is, if the graphic devices are to function as fully for him as reader as all the sound patterns of speech do for him as hearer, there must be some way by which he can

learn to supply with some degree of fullness and accuracy the meanings contributed to speech by the patterns of intonation and stress. As a matter of fact, all of us who read with some maturity and the few who read with extraordinary insight and understanding, do, as they read, carry along and build up such a cumulative comprehension of so much of the total meanings of a discourse that their automatic recognition-responses *fill in the appropriate intonation and stress patterns."*

"Teachers should never allow to pass any oral reading of any sentence that does not display by pitch sequence and stress an understanding of the total meaning." Teachers should demand that the child say the sentence, after it has been "mechanically read," as the child would "talk" it to a companion. Children very soon judge "the significance or the fitness of an intonation sequence, for they are *not*, at the age of five or six, learning to *use* intonation sequences." They have already learned them. Now, in their learning to read, they are simply realizing that "reading" must substitute for the "understanding of talk."

The second stage of the development of reading ability then is complete when the responses to the spelling patterns are so automatic that the contrastive features of the graphic shapes themselves sink below the threshold of attention and the pupil is only conscious of the body of meaning. This consciousness of meaning enables the reader to supply, to produce for materials read "at sight," "those portions of the language signals, the appropriate patterns of intonation and stress that are not represented or only partially represented in the graphic materials given for the eye."

It seems that before the pupil can do what Lefevre wants him to do, the pupil must be able to do what Bloomfield and Fries are most interested in. They are emphasizing the importance of being able to identify the word; they thus have a lot to offer in word identification. Lefevre is more concerned with the total reading act and thus has much to offer in word comprehension. But since context is often invaluable in identifying a word, Lefevre's ideas have meaning also when the pupil cannot identify the word, for unless the word makes sense in the sentence, both in meaning sense and structurally, word identification was faulty.

In the light of the research and experience in the classroom we recommend the following:

1. That pupils learn to associate letter and sound patterns. The relationship emphasized by the linguistic approach is not letter-to-sound, but rather letter patterns to sound patterns.

   The first task is to break the alphabetic code and to grade words according to their phonetic difficulty, not their semantic difficulty. The pupil should be taught to associate specific letters in words with specific sounds through experiencing the whole word in various contexts and lists without conscious analysis of a word into its individual sounds. There should be no analysis of individual sounds as occurs in phonics. Reading should not be confused with the infant's acquisition of speech sounds.

2. That the pupil be taught from the beginning that nearly every generalization has exceptions and that if the word does not make sense in the sentence that he try another approach. We need to teach him flexibility.

3. That the exceptions be taught immediately from the beginning as sight words and that they be clearly labeled as exceptions. The pupil might benefit from some variation; however, this does not mean that he should be exposed to the total range of variation.

The reading program should be flexible enough to include words which are irregular if these words are needed to make the language more meaningful. It should provide contextual settings for words that permit them to be learned in a more natural linguistic environment.[10]

One of the chief objections to phonic and/or linguistic programs has been the limitation that it has put on initial reading materials. Such controlled materials are often viewed as uninteresting and quite meaningless. Edwards,[23] however, notes that adult readers who react negatively to the content of materials in which the vocabulary input is controlled are projecting their own desires for meaning because they have already mastered the decoding process. The beginning reader, on the other hand, is intrigued by the magic of the decoding process. Any student of foreign languages will attest to the thrill of being able to read, "I am big."

Nevertheless, the child's reading vocabulary probably does not need to be controlled to the extent that it now is. The child's early language training in the home is not structured for him. He hears thousands of words and learns to understand and to speak them. His training is sequential only as he makes it so.

The results with individualized reading also tend to indicate that the child learns much more than is formally taught him. He in fact masters that for which he is psychologically, physiologically, and mentally ready.

However, there seems to be value in some control. *We suggest control in his phonic vocabulary* (not in the number of words necessarily but in the rate of introduction of phoneme-phonogram pattern relationships) *so that he will more quickly master the principles that undergird language structure. This control seems sensible only when formally teaching skills of phonic or linguistic analysis. Introducing the pupil to the phonetic consistencies will make him more conscious of the sounds in words, and having learned the principles that guide their relative consistency, he will be able to attack hundreds of words that he has not previously seen in print.*

When a word is met in the child's reading that is alphabetic, it should be taught as such. Thus, if the pupil reads *cat* and he has experienced the *k* sound of *c*, the short *a* sound, and *t*, it should be pointed out to him that the spelling is quite regular. There is no great virtue in teaching this word as a sight word. If in reading he comes across such a word as *come*, it should be taught immediately as a sight word. If the word is actually regular (came), but the child has not yet been formally introduced to such words or to the principles governing the sounding of such a word, the word might simply be pronounced and teaching of the appropriate word-analysis skills might be deferred until later. There is no reason to insist that the child should learn a word as a sight word, or as a configuration, if by application of the principle of pacing, the pupil will soon know it and understand it as a phonetically consistent word.

4. That the best way of breaking the language code may not yet have been developed, but it seems easier to break the code when the child is introduced to words in which the letters behave consistently.

5. That rather than establish a new system in which there is a separate symbol for each sound (such as ITA, or even such a distinctive cueing device as Words in Color) it is better to teach the present system, emphasizing the consistency of sound-symbol patterns and stressing the sound-symbol patterns most often encountered.

6. That the pupil develop the habit of "reading through" words by proceeding from left to right.[32] The order of the letters in a word symbolizes the time-order in which the sounds are made, but it seems far safer to teach the pupil to sound the whole word.

Summary

Neither the configuration nor the phonic method meets the needs of every pupil nor perhaps all the needs of even one pupil. However, since identification of words must be economical, must allow for the greatest amount of transfer, and since it is primarily the process of associating the visual symbol with its oral equivalent, there seems to be a need for the development of a coding system that permits the pupil to attack new words without having to learn a new configuration each time. The teaching of identification skills must make some provision for independence in word attack. *The ultimate goal is self-direction in the learning process.*

The basic contribution of phonics instruction may be that it requires the child to visually study the word. Phonics instruction forces the child to look at the parts of a word and thus may lead to a somewhat different gestalt than is seen if the word were perceived strictly as a unit. The artist sees a picture as a gestalt, but his gestalt is substantially more detailed and refined than that of the casual observer. Through phonics the pupil may learn to scrutinize more adequately the configuration and thus may develop the habit of being unsatisfied with a general, overall view of a word.

It is also apparent that even in the most rigid phonics program a certain number of words will be learned as sight words.

Knowing how to sound out words is also more than just a pronunciation skill. It is an effective way of increasing the child's comprehension vocabulary to the level of his speaking and listening vocabulary.

Durrell and Nicholson[22] point out that ultimate progress in reading is dependent on three factors: (1) The child must notice separate sounds in spoken words; (2) he must be able to see differences in printed letters and words, and (3) he must see the relationships between speech and the written word. He must be able to turn sound symbols into letter symbols and letter symbols into sound symbols. This, we would hope would give the pupil the independence in reading that seems necessary for genuine achievement.

The use of phonics alone does not make a reading program. No amount of phonic training will lead the child to understand the meaning of a written word if the child has never associated an experience with its oral equivalent. Phonics is a method of identifying and recognizing words, and word recognition is only one aspect of the reading process. To be readers children must develop a grasp of meaning, become accurate and independent in identifying words, and want to read.

The pupil who depends totally on configuration skills finds progress increasingly more difficult because his identification problems increase as new words are introduced more and more rapidly. Independence in reading does not seem possible without phonetic and structural analysis skills. Phonics training seems to equip the pupil with one general coding system that fosters development in independence. There are others. Perhaps a few generalizations will clarify our thinking about reading and indeed, about the phonic method.

1. Most children learn to read regardless of the method. Many different methods can and do eventually lead to reading proficiency.
2. There are methods or specific teaching approaches that make a world of difference for the individual child.

3. The method that works best for a given child depends on the individual child. Not all children profit to the same extent from a given method. What is good for slow learners may not work with gifted learners.
4. No one program seems to provide for all the child's reading requirements. The effectiveness of any one approach tends to be increased when it is supplemented by other instructional approaches.
5. The "best" method for most children has both an analytical and a synthetic emphasis. There are few pure-configuration methods, and few programs ignore phonics completely.
6. Some teachers do not make use of the best that is available, but if the teacher is a good teacher, other factors often pale into insignificance. Differences in program effectiveness often can be attributed to teacher effectiveness.
7. A given method may well produce excellent results under one set of conditions but may result in failure under a different set of circumstances.
8. Specific approaches to reading instruction tend to increase children's achievement in certain instructional outcomes but often are weak in other outcomes.

We find it profitable to introduce the child to the phonetic element through the whole word. This does not mean that another approach will not work. It does mean that since reading is a meaningful process the child should keep meaning foremost in his mind. This is best done through a whole-word approach.

From the beginning the child is taught to perceive the sounds in words. He also is taught to notice that some words have the same elements and that they sound alike. Finally, he either infers himself or is taught that he can get to the pronunciation and indirectly to the meaning of a word by noticing the elements in new words and sounding them as he sounded them in other words that he has learned. The pupil must learn that numerous words have some similarity in sound and that he can use this knowledge in attacking other words.

He needs to learn the phoneme-grapheme system by induction rather than by deduction. Rules should grow out of the situations that the pupil deals with. Finally, isolated words should always be brought back into the larger patterns and structures that function linguistically and which carry meaning.

II
DEVELOPING AUDITORY AND VISUAL DISCRIMINATION

To be a reader the pupil must be able to make auditory and visual discriminations. He needs to be able to identify words aurally and visually.

Reading is a twofold process. The reader must identify the symbol and he must be able to associate meaning with it. To identify the printed symbol, he needs to make discriminative visual reactions to the great variety of contrastive symbols on the page. To associate meaning with the symbol, he needs to acquire meanings and to relate the graphic symbol to these previous meanings. This is most readily accomplished if the pupil can associate known speech sounds for which he has meanings with printed letters and letter combinations.

Learning to read is an extension of the speech process. Generally the child already has developed most of the meanings that he encounters in his early reading experiences. He also has associated these meanings or experiences with an aural-oral symbol. Then, teaching this child to read means that the teacher must get him to identify the visual symbol and to associate with it the meaning that he already has associated with a spoken symbol. The child must associate the spoken and written word a sufficient number of times so that he comes to react to the written word with the same meaning that he previously took to the spoken word.

Rarely in English is meaning associated with the written symbol prior to associating it with the spoken symbol. The English language has an alphabet that represents sounds which in turn symbolize meanings. Chinese is an ideographic language in which the written symbols convey meaning directly.

Thus, in learning to read, the spoken word is the familiar stimulus; the written word is the novel stimulus. Gradually, with repeated associations between the written and the spoken word, the child brings to the written word the same meanings that he previously attached to the spoken word. Through association, meaning becomes attached to the written word.

Let us begin our discussion of the auditory and visual skills needed to be a reader with the development of auditory-discrimination skills.

Training in Auditory Discrimination

Auditory discrimination is the ability to discriminate between the sounds or phonemes of a language. It is nothing more than the ability to recognize auditorally that there are sounds which are alike and some that are different. The pupil must be able to identify rhyming words such as *bat* and *rat* and must note the differences in the *c* sound in *cat* and *city*. Whether the pupil will profit from phonics is to a large measure dependent upon his auditory-discrimination skills.

It is evident that auditory discrimination is essential to successful achievement in reading. If the child cannot hear sounds correctly, he normally cannot learn to speak them correctly. A child cannot pronounce distinctions that he cannot hear. Furthermore, if he confuses or distorts sounds in speech, it frequently is impossible for him to associate the correct sound with the visual symbol. Thus, inadequate auditory discrimination leads to improper speech and ultimately to an incorrect association of sound and printed symbol.

The learner must discriminate the phonetic elements that make up a word. He must learn that words consist of sounds, that the same sound may occur in more than one word, and that one word generally has different sounds from those of another word. He must make appropriate associations between the spoken and the written word. And, he gradually needs to realize that words that sound alike frequently look alike.

The ability to make auditory discriminations is greatly lessened by high frequency hearing losses. Berry and Eisenson[6] point out that the high frequency sounds, *f, v, s, z, sh, zh, th, t, d, p, b, k,* and *g,* determine the intelligibility of what is said. If these sounds are not heard correctly, interpretation of what is said becomes more difficult.

Unfortunately, many other children who have not suffered a high-frequency hearing loss are unable to discriminate the sounds necessary for accurate speech. Cole,[14] for example, notes that the average six-year-old is unable to distinguish consistently between the sounds of *g* and *k*, *m* and *n*, and *p* and *b*. This makes it more difficult to learn to read.

Others have identified additional advantages of successful auditory discrimination. Unless the child learns to differentiate between sounds in words, the foundation for phonics is inadequate. Durrell and Murphy[21] report that training in auditory discrimination increases general reading achievement. They note that the child who learns to read easily is usually one who notices the distinct sounds in spoken words.

The facts concerning auditory discrimination are these:

1. Children have varying degrees of ability in auditory discrimination.
2. The maturation of the auditory-discrimination skill is gradual and rarely is fully developed before the age of eight.
3. Poor auditory discrimination is related positively to inaccuracies in articulation and pronunciation and/or to poor achievement in reading.
4. The relationship between auditory discrimination and intelligence is essentially negative.
5. As auditory discrimination matures, the learner becomes capable of producing more and more of the sounds of the language. The child gradually learns to fashion his own speech after the speech that he hears.
6. Auditory discrimination can be developed through instruction.

Some writers[41] suggest that the children whose auditory discrimination is slow in developing might be separately grouped for reading. Groupings based on the pupil's best way of learning or by modality ability might facilitate the task of teaching and enhance learning. Certainly, it would appear that a child with a developmental delay in articulation because of slowness in auditory-discrimination development might benefit from an emphasis on visual learning until he can correct his own articulation errors as he matures.*

The teacher needs to be able to identify the pupil's auditory-discrimination skills. The following instruments are especially helpful in this regard. They provide some measure of the pupil's overall listening and phonic readiness.

———————

* For a more complete discussion of the subject of sensory modalities, and of the tests useful in measuring auditory competency see reference 19.

1. *Stroud-Hieronymus Primary Reading Profiles*, Houghton Mifflin Company. This test is designed for first-second grade level and measures aptitude for reading, auditory association, word recognition, word attack, and interpretation and comprehension. Test 1, *Aptitude for Reading*, is a listening test, requiring no reading of any kind. Its purpose is to indicate the pupil's aptitude to understand spoken language and directions as well as his ability to associate the meaning of pictures with what he hears.

2. *Botel Reading Inventory*, Follett Publishing Company. This inventory for grades one to twelve has a section entitled "Word Opposites Listening Test." There are ten multiple-choice items at each level. Each item consists of four or five words, and the pupil must find a word in each line that is the opposite of the first word.

3. *Sequential Tests of Educational Progress: Listening*, Cooperative Test Division, Educational Testing Service. This listening test is part of a larger battery of tests usable on grade levels four to fourteen.

4. *Brown-Carlsen Listening Comprehension Test*, Harcourt, Brace & World. This test for grade 9 to adult measures five important listening skills— immediate recall, following directions, recognizing transitions, recognizing word meanings, and lecture comprehension.

5. *Durrell-Sullivan Reading Capacity Test*, Harcourt, Brace & World. This test for grades 2.5 to 6 requires from thirty to forty-five minutes. It measures word and paragraph meanings, spelling, and written recall. It requires no reading and is basically a listening comprehension test.

6. *The Illinois Test of Psycholinguistic Abilities*, Institute for Research on Exceptional Children, University of Illinois.

7. *Mills Learning Methods Test*, Mills Center, Fort Lauderdale, Florida.

8. *Roswell-Chall Auditory Blending Test*. Essay Press, P.O. Box 5, Planetarium Station, New York, New York.

9. *California Phonics Survey Test*, California Test Bureau.

10. *Auditory Discrimination Test*, Language Research Associates, Box 95, 950 East 59th Street, Chicago, Illinois.

11. *Leavell Hand-Eye Coordination Test*, Keystone View Company.

12. *Perceptual Forms Test*, Winter Haven Lions Publications Committee, P.O. Box 1045, Winter Haven, Florida.

13. *Phonics Knowledge Survey*, Bureau of Publications, Columbia University.

14. *Phonics Mastery Test*, Follett Publishing Company.

15. *Robbins Speech Sound Discrimination and Verbal Imagery Type Tests*. Expression Company, Magnolia, Massachusetts.

16. *McKee Inventory of Phonetic Skills*. Houghton Mifflin Company.

17. *Marianne Frostig Developmental Test of Visual Perception*. Consulting Psychologists Press, Palo Alto, California.

The following techniques may prove helpful in teaching auditory discrimination. The child should be tested on each of these exercises. The teacher should drill him only on those aspects that he has not mastered. Some of these exercises are proper only after the child has begun to read.

1. Check gross discriminations for sounds; for example, the voices of specific children; taps on the desk, the radiator, or a bell; songs of a bird, the call of a cow, the chirping of a grasshopper, the neigh of a horse; the various sounds of a rhythm band. Each instrument may be associated with a physical activity such as skipping, laughing, clapping of the hands, or tiptoeing.
2. List the names of children beginning with the same sound. Ask children to give other words beginning with the same sound.
3. Have children note similarities or differences in the initial consonants of pairs of words; for example, the similarities in *can* and *cat* and the differences in *cat* and *bat*.

    Picture exercises are especially beneficial here. The child is shown three pictures, the first of which may be that of a bell. Of the other two pictures, the name of only one begins with *b*. The teacher asks the pupil to pick out the one that begins with the same sound as *bell* and to draw a line to it.
4. Provide the pupils with three pictures and ask them to pick out the two pictures whose names begin with the same sound.

5. Give each child two picture cards. One card has the beginning or rhyming sound like a picture on the chalk ledge. Each child in turn places his card on the ledge that has the same sound as the picture on the ledge. Another variation is to put many cards on the ledge and let each child pick up a card that has the same beginning sound that the teacher has. At a later stage the letter symbol can be used with the picture cards. Picture sets are available through Ginn and Company and through the Ideal School Supply Company.

6. After demonstrating the *b* sound, for example, ask pupils to provide words with *b* that answer questions like the following:
   a. What do you use to hit a ball?
   b. In what do you sleep?
   c. What word do you use when you want to say that something is large?

7. After demonstrating a given sound, for example, *f*, present the pupils with a mimeographed page of pictures. Ask them to put a line through the objects whose names do not begin with an *f*. The page may contain pictures of a hat, fox, foot, box, cat, hammer, finger, fan, and file.

8. Explain the meaning of rhyme and illustrate it by providing words that actually rhyme, such as *am, ham, jam, Pam, ram* or *at, hat, mat, Pat, cat, rat, fat*.

9. Ask children to provide rhymes for simple words such as *cat, bet, lit, lot, but*. The game "Quiz Panel"[44] is quite adaptable to this task. The teacher selects a panel of four pupils who sit in the front of the room. He pronounces a word and individual members of the panel must provide a rhyming word. When the panel member misses, he is replaced by another member of the class. A variant form of this exercise asks the child to do picture-reading. The child is shown three pictures, the first of which is a picture of a bat. Of the other two pictures, only one rhymes with *bat*. The teacher asks him to pick out the one that rhymes with *bat*.

10. Suggest three words, two of which rhyme. Ask children to pick out the word that does not rhyme with the other two words. Two small booklets entitled *Rhyming* are available from Continental Press, Inc., for teaching teaching rhyming skills. The booklets contain twenty-four lessons.

11. Ask children to note similarities and differences in final consonants of pairs of words.

12. Have children listen for and give words beginning or ending with the same consonant blend or speech consonant. The order should be (1) beginning consonant blend, (2) final consonant blend, (3) initial speech consonant, and (4) final speech consonant.

13. Have children listen for and give monosyllabic words containing the same short vowel.

14. Have children listen for and give monosyllabic words containing the same long vowel.

15. Have children listen for and give words of two or more syllables.

16. Have children circle the word that rhymes with the name of picture.

17. Have children associate consonant sounds with the appropriate visual symbol. The child identifies each picture, says its name, and then locates the letter which symbolizes the beginning sound of the picture.

Training in Visual Discrimination*

Surely one of the most important skills needed for reading is the ability to visually analyze and synthesize printed words. The pupil must be able to work out and to distinguish differences between visual stimuli. He must be able to note similarities and differences in the form of objects, pictures, geometric figures, letters, and words. Generally children by the time they begin school have learned to discriminate between gross figures and objects. They see the differences between a cat and a dog and between circles, triangles, and

---

* For a discussion of such aspects as visual adequacy, visual deficiencies, symptoms of eye disturbances, and visual screening tests, see reference 19.

squares. They also have learned something about words. Long before they come to school they have identified signs such as PHILLIPS 66, STOP, WICHITA, or KANSAS. They have noted that some words are long and others short, that some have ascending letters and others have descending letters, and that some words look alike and that others look different. They may not yet be able to discriminate *b* from *d* or *these* from *those*.

Unfortunately, it is not always possible to know whether the pupil has used the correct process in identifying a word. Unless he has identified the word through some peculiarity of the word itself, he may not have learned or at least has learned incorrectly. Children frequently learn to identify a word by a simple association process. Perhaps the word STOP is STOP only when it is seen at the end of a block and appears on an octagonal-shaped figure. The word BOB is BOB only when it appears on that card with the dirt splotch in the bottom left-hand corner.

Thus the question arises, What should the teacher emphasize in visual discrimination training?

Ever since there has been concern with identifying the factors that were indicative of both reading readiness and achievement, visual discrimination has been accorded a primary position. Gradually, concern focused on those specific visual discrimination tasks that are most predictive of reading readiness. Researchers identified the importance of visual discrimination of letters or words from the beginning. Some emphasized shape-matching or the matching of animal pictures or geometric forms, but other evidence indicated that this had little transfer value to word discrimination.

A series of studies at Boston University[20] suggests that most children are able to match one capital letter with another capital letter and one lowercase letter with another.

Barrett[5] found that being able to discriminate, recognize, and name letters and numbers was the best single predictor, but pattern-copying and word-matching were strongly related to first-grade reading achievement. However, other factors (auditory discrimination, language facility, story sense) still contributed as much or more to the prediction of first-grade reading.

In a later study Barrett[4] found that recognition of letters had the highest relationship with beginning-reading achievement; discrimination of beginning sounds had the next highest relationship, but ending sounds in words, shape completion, ability to copy a sentence, and discrimination of vowel sounds in words were also positively related.

Wheelock and Silvaroli[53] found a significant difference in visual-discrimination ability among kindergarten children from high and low socioeconomic groups, and their study indicated that the ability to make instant responses of recognition to the capital letters can be taught. The children from the lower extreme of the socioeconomic continuum seemed to profit most from the training.

There is no doubt that reading requires the ability to distinguish each word from every other word. It also seems apparent that the pupil must be relatively more skilled in noting the differences among words than in noting the similarities.

One cannot infer that all matching is useless. Some children may not have learned this simple step. The teacher uses a matching exercise as a diagnostic device. When the pupil has not developed adequately in this regard he should stress matching of objects, signs, and words. He starts teaching at the level the child has attained. The child must learn matching to the extent that he consistently responds to *b* as *b* or to *was* as *was*.

Certain other principles should guide the teacher in his teaching of visual discrimination. He must be careful not to overdrill on any one skill. If the pupil can do a specific exercise with ease, it is imperative that with him the teacher must work on a higher-level skill. There perhaps is no quicker way to destroy interest in learning to read than to force the pupil to engage in a readiness activity that he already has mastered.

The teacher also needs to develop some sequence in teaching the letters. He must begin with simple forms and proceed to more difficult ones. Some letters are readily distinguishable, for example, *x* and *b*. Others are not so readily distinguished. Children have a tendency to confuse *b* and *d*, *p* and *b*, *p* and *d*, *p* and *q*, *u* and *n*, *m* and *w*, *o* and *e*, *o* and *c*, *e* and *c*, and *g* and *b*. These letters profitably might be introduced at different times to minimize interference.

In recent years there has been an emphasis on the use of colored symbols to differentiate the phonemes of the language, and research data indicate that color is a definite aid to visual perception among kindergarten children.

Finally, in visual-discrimination exercises, the emphasis is not on reading. We do not specifically teach the pupil to associate a printed word with a spoken word or with an object or experience. The pupil must note differences in words. He should be able to verbalize the differences in the words. He should be able to verbalize the difference in the initial letter, the final letter, or in the general form of the words. We expect to teach him "what to look for," so he may identify words as distinct units of language.

A desirable sequence of exercises in visual discrimination has not been identified. In many instances it has not been possible to develop exercises that are distinct from tests of intelligence. The following exercises are merely suggestive of some activities that may be used to develop discrimination between words, syllables, and letters:

1. Check on the pupil's discrimination of gross form; pictures, objects, and geometric figures, differences in color; or ability to fit the the pieces of a puzzle. The child may have to learn the blues or the reds in sweaters, dresses, and trousers worn by his classmates. He may learn to distinguish various shades of green in nature. And he may learn to mix colors so as to produce various shades.

   Children should learn to trace a design, to visualize spatial relationships, and to think and reason spatially; they must develop eye-hand coordination and visual-motor skills. It is believed by many that reversals are errors in visual and spatial location.

   Four small books, *Visual Discrimination*, Level 1 and Level 2, and *Visual-Motor Skills*, Level 1 and Level 2, are available from Continental Press, Inc. Each booklet contains twenty-four lessons and teaches visual motor and spatial skills.

2. Present each pupil with a copy of his name. Let him note the differences and similarities between his name and that of some of his classmates.

   An exercise of this type teaches gross discrimination in word forms. Exercises similar to the following teach the same skill.

   Encircle the word that is different.

cat	cry	cat		boy	bed	bed		car	her	car
day	yes	yes		fly	bee	fly		and	why	and

   Put a line under the two words that are alike.

yes	yes		see	fell		mat	met
cat	bat		saw	saw		rat	bat
on	no		fan	pan		in	on

3. Provide each pupil with a mimeographed page of letters and/or monosyllabic words that are arranged in columns by pairs. Let him encircle those pairs that are different.

An exercise of this type teaches gross discrimination in letters. The following exercises call for the same type of skill.

Encircle the letter that is different.

s	s	k		m	l	m		p	p	b
h	y	h		n	m	n		s	s	a
b	b	d		r	r	z		n	n	v

Color the feathers in the indian headdress on which there is a word that begins with the same letter as the letter in the feather on the right.

Draw a line between the two letters that are alike.

b	a		k	t		v	t		s	s		r	h
c	b		t	l		h	t		a	z		b	b

Draw a line from each word to the letter that is the same as the letter that begins the word.

x	bat	b		bib	t
	hat	p		hen	h
	map	t		mop	n
	net	h		nut	p
	pan	m		pet	m
	top	n		tub	b

4. Present three words and let the pupil select the word that is repeated more than once in the sequence; for example, *can*, *pan*, *can*. By increasing the number of words to five the task is made more difficult.

5. Present three words and let the pupil select the two words that have the same beginning consonant, the same ending consonant, or the same two-letter beginning or ending consonant.
6. Present three words and let the pupil select the two words that have the same vowel.
7. Present three words and let the pupil select the two polysyllabic words. One of the words should be monosyllabic.

Developing a Knowledge of the Alphabet

An important visual-discrimination skill is the ability to discriminate between the letters of the alphabet. Studies suggest that a knowledge of the names of the letters of the alphabet may be one of the best predictors of a child's readiness for reading. They also indicate that the ability to write letters dictated and to identify the letters named are important indicators of first-grade reading achievement.

We can only surmise what the reason for this finding might be, but a child who has associated a name with a letter already has learned basic reading skills. He has associated some meaning with a printed symbol and he has learned to discriminate it visually from other forms.

Whereas the studies do not indicate that the pupil should be able to name all the letters or that he should know them in alphabetical order, this knowledge is not without value. Eventually, the pupil will find it necessary to file his words, to locate them, and to use the picture dictionary.

The names of both capital and small letters should be taught first, but from the start the pupil should realize that each letter both has a name and represents a sound. Some children will have learned to identify letters and to name them by the time they enter kindergarten. Others will have to be taught in school.

The following techniques may prove helpful in teaching the names and sounds of the letters:

1. Let each child become familiar with the specific letters used in his name. Point out the similarities and differences among the letters and tell him that these marks are called letters. Some pupils will learn to differentiate capital and lowercase letters at this level.
2. Tell the child that the little marks or letters in his name have names. Begin teaching of names with a few letters at a time.
3. Identify each letter with a key word: *b* with *bee*; *c* with *cat*; *s* with *sun*. Teach the pupil that each letter also has a sound.

4. Let each child trace the specific letters being studied. After some practice, ask him to reproduce it from memory. The name of the letter should be said while he is tracing the letter.
5. Expose the pupil to ABC books, letter cards, and picture dictionaries. Demonstrate that the reason the sounds at the beginning and end of words are alike is due to the fact that they have the same letter at the beginning or at the end.
6. Teach the pupil that the same name is given to two different manuscript or printed forms: the capital letter and the lowercase letter.
7. Let the pupil arrange the letter cards in alphabetical order, beginning with a few letters at a time.
8. Ask the pupil to locate or arrange words in an alphabetical list.

Training in Left-to-Right Progression

Another skill related to visual discrimination is the ability to place letters in proper sequence in a word. This is a new concept for young children. They have not been taught to observe directions in their everyday perceptions. A dog looks like a dog whether the eye movement is from left to right or from right to left. Unfortunately, in reading a word this is not so. The letters *s a w* read from left to right say *saw*, but read from right to left say *was*. Thus, one of the first requirements in learning to read is the learning of new habits of perception. The child must perceive from left to right.

The term commonly used to indicate that the child is making the wrong directional attack on words is *reversing*.

There are two major points of view as to the origin of reversals. One, represented by Orton,[43] suggests that reversals result from lack of cerebral dominance and are prime factors in reading disability. Another point of view suggests that reversals are a universal phenomenon and do not necessarily cause poor reading. This view suggests that they indicate an unfamiliarity with the symbols that the child is trying to learn. Studies also indicate that reversals may be caused by lack of maturation, visual defects, the habit of perceiving objects from right to left, overemphasizing the final sounds of words by concentrating on word families, and the exclusive use of the configuration method. If a word is taught to the child as a gestalt or as a total configuration, the child has no need to differentiate between right and left. The word will be the same and he can "read" it if he remembers its sound and meaning.

During the early school years reversals have been considered to be normal phenomena. Unfortunately, this assumption may have hindered progress in working with the difficulties. Reversals certainly become a serious problem in reading when they continue beyond the second or third grade. After those years children who reverse generally do not make normal progress in reading.

Reversals are of various kinds. Children may reverse certain letters, such as *b* for *d* or *p* for *q*. They may read an entire word backward, such as *was* for *saw*. Or they may alter the position of certain letters in words, such as *aminal* for *animal*. We thus speak of static reversals, kinetic reversals, and instances of transposition.

The elimination of reversals in reading is not easy. No one method has proved completely effective. In the following exercises we have attempted to suggest some that are suitable both for prereaders and for children at higher levels.

1. Teach children the meaning of left and right by showing them the difference between their right and their left hand or by playing the game "Simon Says." Here the child receives an oral direction sometimes with and sometimes without the words, "Simon Says." When the direction is not preceded by these words and the child carries out the direction, the child is out of the game. The teacher's directions should emphasize distinctions between right and left : "Put your right foot forward." Raise your left hand."

   Teachers in the Napa, California, Kindergarten project[16] have found that when children are taught the *b* and *p* with the letters which circle to the right (B, P, J, j, p, b, h, m, n, r) and when *d* and *q* are taught with letters which circle to the left (c, a, d, q, e, f) that reversals have been almost completely eliminated. Part of the pupil's problems is the discovery of what the ciritical dimensions of difference are such as "curve left," "curve right," and "obliqueness."[35]

2. Ask the child to draw an arrow pointing to the right under the first letter of a word.

3. In arranging a series of pictures into a narrative sequence the child should be required to follow a left-to-right sequence.

4. Point out to pupils that the left side of a word is the beginning of that word and that the right side is the end of that word.

5. Use mechanical devices such as the Controlled Reader to demonstrate the reading sequence. This particular machine permits thought units to appear in a left-to-right sequence.

6. In referring to a line of print, to a caption under a picture, or to written directions on the bulletin board, sweep the hand from left to right while indicating that in reading this is the required direction.

7. Demonstrate to children how meaning is distorted when the word is read from right to left. "Jim was in the barn" is quite different from "Jim saw in the barn." Some success may be obtained by teaching the child what a reversal is, how it is made, and what the results look like.

8. Let children engage in left-to-right tracing exercises. Initially these are finger tracing exercises; crayons and pencils may be used later. These exercises also develop skill in staying on a line or in making an accurate return sweep. The child may trace a line, numbers, words, and strokes, or he may draw geometric figures in left-to-right progression. The "reading" of the calendar also is helpful in developing the left-to-right skill.

9. In demonstrating left-to-right progression in monosyllabic words, put each letter in a block and number the blocks in a left-to-right direction.

10. Require the pupil to write only one word on a line. The first letter is placed at the extreme left edge of the paper.

11. Require the pupil to cover the word with a card and move it slowly to the right, thus exposing one letter at a time in a left-to-right progression. The same process may be followed in reading an entire line of print.

12. Let the pupil engage in choral reading, provide alphabetizing and dictionary exercises, and let him use the typewriter.

13. Demonstrate to children that by changing the *d* to *b* in the word *dad* it becomes *bad*. Children should learn that words are pronounced in a left-to-right direction and that this is done by beginning with the first letter. Ask them to form other words from a list of given words by changing the first letter.

14. Let the pupil trace a word written in manuscript or cursive script. As he traces the word, he should speak out each part of the word.

    Some authorities suggest that there must be finger contact while tracing; others, that there should be pencil contact. The child continues this until he can reproduce the form from memory. He should have met the word in a reading context, and eventually files the word in an alphabetical file. Another method has the child write the word as the teacher speaks the sounds of the word in a left-to-right progression.

15. After the child has learned to read and can handle the alphabet, the teacher may want to check the pupil on a list of words similar to the one below. Each word, if reversed, will make a different word.

nab	net	pit	mad	tug	pal
bat	pin	top	den	gum	ram
bin	bun	bad	dog	wed	rap
but	on	bag	nod	won	rat
pan	Pam	Mac	dot	bus	saw
mat	tap	cod	bud	gas	

Summary

Chapter II examined the importance of auditory and visual discrimination skills for reading and then suggested ways of helping the pupil to develop skill in these areas. In a way, Chapter II is the foundation of the remaining chapters. The pupil can learn beginning consonant sounds, vowel sounds, end consonant sounds, and all the other sounds, which are the content of subsequent chapters, only if he can auditorially discriminate them; he can learn to read only if he can identify the printed symbols and can discriminate one from another. The basis for the development of a coding system is adequate training in visual and auditory discrimination.

III

TEACHING THE BEGINNING
CONSONANT SOUNDS

INITIAL reading exercises are designed to develop a basic recognition vocabulary. In working toward this goal the pupil is asked to do several things:

1. To do picture-reading.
2. To associate sounds with the whole word.
3. To use the context both for identifying the word and for understanding its meaning.
4. To learn the names of the individual letters.
5. To write the letters.
6. To associate sounds with the beginning consonant and with the median vowel.

Point six is our concern in this chapter. The pupil must learn to hear sounds in words and to see phonograms or to notice the letter or letters that represent the sounds of whole words.

The major aim in this initial stage of teaching reading is to teach the consonants in the beginning position. The child needs to learn what is meant when the teacher says, "This word begins with an *m, t, b, h, p,* or *n* sound." He must also learn to deal with consonant substitution. He needs to learn what changing of the initial consonant does to the sound and the meaning of the words.

For years, educators have debated the question whether consonants or vowels should be introduced first. Perhaps the question is invalid. If pupils are to begin with complete words, and this is our emphasis in this book, consonants and vowels must necessarily be introduced concomitantly. The reasons for systematic and formal studying of consonants first usually include the following:

1. There is a greater correspondence between the consonant sounds and the letters used to represent them than between the vowel sounds and the

letters used to represent them. Fifteen consonants ($b, f, h, j, k, l, m, n, p, r, t,$ $v, w, y,$ and z) have usually one sound each.

2. Consonant letters are more significant in the perceptual image of a word; (thus, j–hnn–– h–t th– b–s–b–ll is more readily identified than –o–––ie –i– ––e –a–e–a––.) McKee[40] notes that if the pupil knows letter-sound associations for the consonants and if he understands that each printed word in his reading matter is one which makes sense in the context, the pupil can do a lot of independent reading without having been taught letter-sound associations for vowels. McKee adds that the pupil cannot possibly read much if he knows letter-sound associations for vowels, but does not know them for consonants.

3. Consonant letters to a great degree determine the sound of the vowel; whereas vowels rarely affect the sound of the consonant. Thus, in one-syllable words a single vowel is usually short when it is in the beginning of a word, or in the middle position and followed only by a consonant.

4. Most of the words encountered in beginning reading begin with consonants.

5. It makes sense to have the child work through the word from left to right, and this means beginning with the first letter, which commonly is a consonant.

During the first phase of the child's experience with linguistic phonics the pupil should learn how to sound the common consonants. Many children will have mastered all the skills required at this level in the readiness program. They can name most letters and have associated the appropriate sound with the letters. For others, teaching tasks remain.

The Order of Priority in Sounds

Not all consonants can be made with the same ease or facility. There is some order of priority in sounds. The Institute of Logopedics at the University of Wichita uses the term "order of primitivity" to refer to the order of the development of the sounds in the language. This order is $m, p, b, t, d, n, h, w, f, v, k, g, th, sh, zh, ch, j, s, z, r,$ and l. The mechanics of the articulatory process developed physiologically from the integration of the basic chewing, sucking, swallowing, and similar vegetative reflexes. Experience shows that when a child suffers a speech loss, the loss is in reverse order. The last sounds to be developed are the first sounds to be lost.

Many errors in reading arise from the fact that children cannot or do not discriminate certain sounds orally and consequently neither make the sound properly nor form the proper association between the spoken element and the written element. The teacher must determine what phonetic elements should be taught, in what order they should be taught, and how they might be taught best.

There are stages in the development of general reading skills, of word-attack skills, and of specific phonic skills. The teacher must know what the goals of achievement are at each level for each of these. He must realize that children progress at different rates through various levels and that they differ from one another in the levels they ultimately attain. This makes the identification of a natural sequence in teaching phonic skills even more important.

The sequence, whatever it may be, should not be used for the setting of definite standards of attainment for all children, but rather for the guidance of teachers in their attempt to provide for individual differences. Each child must be led through the sequence at a rate at which he can succeed. Thus, there really are no first-grade skills. There is only a sequence of skills through which children normally should proceed. This sequence the teacher must identify.

Word-recognition skills are important. Proper training in them increases independence of attacking words, improves comprehension, and leads to more accurate pronunciations. Perhaps as significant is the fact that they are not acquired in a year or two. Training needs to be continuous, it needs to be applied in many situations, and it needs to be sequential.

Davis[17,45] reports that some six-year-old children have not mastered *l, r, s, th, sh, zh, z,* and *wh*. Van Riper and Butler[51] report that most of the articulatory errors made by primary children involve *f, l, r, s, sh, k, th,* and *ch*, and that elementary children have most difficulty with *r, s, l, th*. Hildreth[32] points out that the *k, q, v, x, y,* and *z* should be introduced last.

There are other reasons for not using certain letters in initial phonic (and possibly reading) exercises. The letter *x*, for example, represents six distinct sounds. It has the sound of *ks* in *box*, of *gz* in *exist*, of *gsh* in *anxious*, of *gzh* in *luxurious*, of *z* in *xylophone*, and of *gksh* in *anxious* (angshus). The letter *q* occurs only with *u* and then has the sound of *kw*. The letter *k* is readily confused with the much more used hard *c*.

Because of these data the following letters might best be excluded from early *phonic* experiences: *k, q, v, x, y, z*. There is no great advantage in introducing them. Relatively few words use these sounds.

A word like *you* may be taught as a sight word. This does not mean that these sounds are not introduced in the first grade. Some youngsters may be able to handle them almost immediately. Appendix I lists the multiple spellings of the various consonant sounds and also gives a description of the sounds that given consonant letters can symbolize.

The letters themselves present problems for the pupil. Popp[46] found that the most frequently confused pairs of letters in rank order by nonreading kindergarteners were *p-q, d-b, d-q, d-p, b-p, h-u, i-l, k-y, t-u, c-e, d-h, h-n, h-y, j-k,* and *n-u.* Coleman[15] found that *p-q* and *d-b* were more often confused by preschoolers than they were correctly identified.

Steps in Teaching Beginning Consonants

Teaching beginning consonants basically involves the development of auditory, visual, and kinesthetic discrimination of the sound. Teaching the initial *b* sound, for example, consists of the following steps:

1. The teacher may pronounce some words that begin with the *b* sound such as *bat, bib, bug, boy.* The *b* sound may be slightly elongated or stressed, but it should not be distorted. The child may also be taught the mouth geography of the sound. For a description of how to teach this, consult Appendix II. And, it is useful to identify each sound with a little jingle.

B b	**C c**	**D d**
Boys, boys,*	Cat, cat,*	Dog, dog,*
Let's have some fun,	Your purr is sweet,	Chew your bone.
Come out and play	But you have stickers	That will keep you
When your work is done.	In your feet.	Close at home.

   The teacher should be careful that the initial association that the child makes is between the sound of a whole word with either a picture or a printed word.
2. The teacher asks the pupils what they noticed about the initial sound. Were the initial sounds alike or different?
3. The teacher pronounces words, some of which begin with a *b* sound and some of which do not. The pupils raise their hand when the word begins with the *b* sound.
4. The pupils give other words beginning with a *b* sound. The teacher may accept any word which begins with a *b*. Such combinations as *br* are

---

* Courtesy of Avis Griffith, Lillian Peak, and Dorothy M. Randle.

acceptable at this stage. The teacher may ask if there is any one in the class whose name begins with a *b* sound.

5. The teacher prints the letter *b* on the blackboard and writes out words such as *bed, bat, bib, bug,* or any other word beginning with a *b* that the youngsters mentioned. He may put pictures on the chalkboard to make the lesson more meaningful, and the pupils may be asked to pronounce the name of the pictured objects. It is useful to have key pictures for each of the sounds to be taught. The teacher may associate the *b* with a picture of a bed and call it "the bed sound." The pupils may be asked to come to the blackboard and draw a line around any pictures whose names begin with the *b* sound. In this and the following exercises the pupil gradually learns to associate a letter with a name and with the sound that he hears at the beginning of words like *bat, bed,* or *book.*

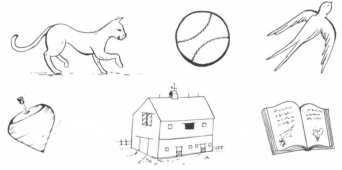

6. The teacher writes a name under each picture whose name begins with *b*.

bell   **boy**

7. The pupils are told to look carefully at the letter beginning each of the words under the pictures, and the teacher gives the letter a name. The teacher again sounds the words making sure that the pupils listen carefully to the sound at the beginning of each word.

8. The pupils next are taught to associate the *b* sound with both the capital and lowercase letter *b*. They may be shown that a word like *Ben,* which begins with a capital letter, is sounded in the beginning just like the word

bed. It is helpful to show the pupils that if a personal name begins with *b*, the capital *B* must be used.

9. The pupils then read the words in unison.

10. The pupils next print the letter *b*, both capital and lowercase.

Workbook and other teacher-prepared materials may then be used to teach the consonant sounds and the technique of consonant substitution. The following exercises are illustrative:

1. Look at the pictures below. Say the name of each picture. Note that each begins like the key word *bed.*

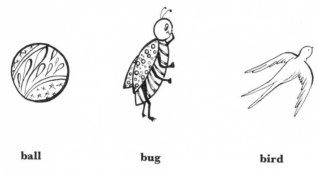

ball   **bug**   **bird**

2. Put a line through each picture that begins like *bed.*

3. Draw a line from the letter *t* to the pictures whose names begin with the same sound.

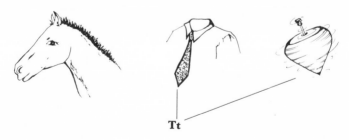

Tt

This exercise helps the pupil to associate the *t* sound with both the capital and lowercase letter *t*. The pupil should say the name of the picture so that he gradually develops the concept that words that sound alike initially have the same letter at the beginning.

As soon as the pupil has mastered more than one consonant, exercises such as the following are helpful.

1. Have the pupil draw a line through the two pictures in each row that begin with the same sound.

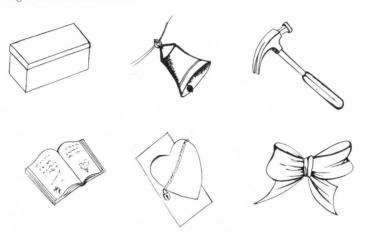

2. Have pupils circle each word that begins like the name of the picture.

bat   **cat**   **hog**   **bug**

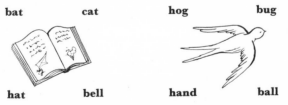

hat   **bell**   **hand**   **ball**

3. Have the pupils write or circle the proper consonant in various types of exercises.

   a. In the following exercise the pupil has to write the proper consonant on the line.

   1. _____ **is the**   **2.** _____ **is the**
   sound that starts   **sound that starts**

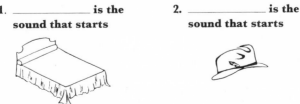

b. Have the pupil circle the correct beginning letter sound.

b   **b**
h   **d**
m   **h**

c. Have the pupil write under each picture the initial consonant of the name of each picture.

___ **ate**   ___ **ow**   ___**ear**

Another variant of this exercise is the following: It requires the pupil to write out the entire word.

_____   _____   _____

4. Make a circular card similar to the one below. Write the ending on the card and put the initial consonants on a strip of paper. The pupil pulls the strip of paper through the opening revealing new words.[31]

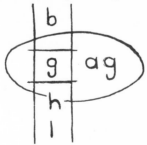

5. Have the pupil draw a line from words which have the same ending, but which begin with different consonants, to the picture which the word represents. This teaches that changing the beginning consonant alters the meaning of the word.

bat

cat

hat

rat

6. Have the pupil circle the word that gives meaning to the sentence and that agrees with the picture at the end of the line.

a. The pup bit the fan.
·man.

b. The can is hot.
pan

7. Have the pupil fill in the blank in the sentence with one of the letters at the end of the sentence, thus giving meaning to the sentence.
   a. The pup___ it the man.   (h, b)
   b. Ben has a pet ___ en.   (h, b)

The Letters B, C, D, G, H, J, M, N, P, T, W

We have already suggested that it might help to introduce sounds in a given order. Although the teaching of any consonant follows the procedures outlined above, some sounds might be deferred for later teaching because they are more difficult to sound. Table I lists some monosyllabic words containing short vowels that are helpful in teaching the consonants *b*, *c* (sounded *k*), *d*, *g*, *h*, *j*, *m*, *n*, *p*, *t*, and *w* in the beginning position.

As a result of this linguistic approach, the pupil should gradually develop a sense of the structure of words. When words are organized into linguistic spelling patterns,[42] as seen in Table II, the pupil should see words not as sight words but as words having a similar structure.

TABLE I

MONOSYLLABIC WORDS FORMED BY B, C, D, G, H, J, M, N, P, T, AND W

bad	cab	dad	gab	had	jab	Mac
bag	cam	Dad	gad	ham	jag	mad
ban	can	dam	gag	hem	jam	man
bat	cap	Dan	gap	hen	Jan	map
bed	cat	den	get	hid	Jed	mat
bet	cob	did	God	him	jet	men
bib	cod	dig	got	hit	jib	met
bid	cog	dim	gum	hog	jig	Mig
big	con	din	gun	hop	Jim	mob
bin	cop	dip	gut	hot	job	mop
bit	cot	Doc		hub	jog	mud
bog	cud	don		hum	jug	mum
bud	cup	Don		hut	jut	
Bud	cut	dot				

nab	pad	pig	tab	tin	was (wäz)	
nag	Pam	pin	tag	tip	web	
Nan	pan	Pip	tam	Tip	wed	
nap	pat	pit	tan	tit-tat	wet	
Ned	Pat	pop	tap	Tom	wig	
net	peg	pot	tat	ton (tən)	win	
nib	Peg	pun	Ted	top	wit	
nip	pen	pup	ten	tot	won (wən)	
nod	pep	put (pùt)	tic	tub		
not	pet		Tim	tug′		
nub				tut		
nun						
nut						

For lists of two-syllable words to illustrate and teach the phonic skills as they function in multisyllabic words, see Appendix IV.

The Letters F, L, R, S

Having mastered the eleven consonants suggested above, the pupil might next be introduced to words containing the *f*, *l*, *r*, and *s* sounds. Teachers will find that children generally have much more difficulty articulating these sounds than those that have been considered previously. In some instances it is absolutely necessary to teach the placement in the mouth (the mouth geography)* for each sound. The child must be taught the lip and tongue position required in making the sound. Adding these four sounds, *f, l, r,* and *s,* to the pupil's repertoire permits the teacher to introduce many additional phonetically consistent words. You will notice, however, from Table III that many of these monosyllabic words are not consistent.

TABLE II

WORD STRUCTURE

	a	*e*	*i*	*o*	*u*
b	bat	bet	bit		but
c	cat			cot	cut
d				dot	
f	fat		fit		
g		get		got	gut
h	hat		hit	hot	hut
j		jet		jot	jut
k			kit		
l		let	lit	lot	
m	mat	met	mitt		
n	Nat	net		not	nut
p	pat	pet	pit	pot	
r	rat			rot	rut
s	sat	set	sit		
t	tat			tot	
v	vat	vet			
w		wet	wit		
y		yet			

There needs to be specific teaching of each of the following:

1. The words in Table II introduce additional *a* sounds: the *a* (ȯ) sound in *all, call, fall, gall, ball,* and *wall,* and the *a* (ä) sound in *bar, car, far, jar, mar, par,* and *tar.* The pupil should note that *a* followed by *r* in monosyllable words is the *ä* sound. These words may be learned as the "car" words. When *a* is followed by *ll,* it has the *ȯ* sound, and the words may be identified as the "all" words. These variant sounds of *a* should not be taught until the pupil has mastered the short sounds of the vowels.

2. The pupil also must learn that quite commonly monosyllabic words ending in an *f, l,* and *s* sound double the final consonant letter.** He must learn that in these words only one written letter is pronounced and that in spelling he must use two letters to reproduce the sound.

---

* See Appendix I.

** Exceptions to this rule are *as, bus, clef, gas, has, his, if, is, nil, of, pal, plus, pus, this, thus, was, yes, beef, dwarf, golf, half, loaf, mail, meal, roof, self, soil, thief, wheel,* and *wolf.*

3. Words ending in double *ll* preceded by *u* sometimes are pronounced as *u̇* and sometimes as short *u* sound: thus *bull, full, pull*, but also *cull, dull, gull, hull, lull, mull*, and *null*. For this reason *full* and *pull* may be introduced as sight words at this level of phonic development.

4. Even though the *ər* sound as in *cur* and the *ȯ* sound as in *for* and *boss* are listed in the vocabulary in Table II, these sounds should not be introduced at this time. Thus, the words *her* and *for* should be introduced as sight words. The words *log, of, war, son*, and *was* must also be learned as sight words.

5. The letter *s* frequently is pronounced as a *z*. We have listed some of these words: *as, has, his, is, was*. The pronouncing of *s* as *z* generally occurs (1) at the end of some monosyllabic words (as, has, his, is, was), (2) when the *s* occurs between two vowels, and (3) after *j, s, x, z, sh, zh*, and *ch*, the *s* is an *es*; after *f, k, p, t*, and unvoiced *th*, the *s* is simply an *s*; after all other consonants the *s* is a *z*.

TABLE III

MONOSYLLABIC WORDS FORMED BY B, C, D, F, G, H, J, L, M, N, P, R, S, T, W
AND THE SHORT VOWELS

as (az)	for (fȯr)	leg	pus	rot	sin
bus	fun	let	rag	rub	sip
cur (kər)	fir (fər)	lid	ram	rug	sir (sər)
fad	fur (fər)	lip	ran	rum	sit
fag	gas	lit	rap	run	sob
fan	Gus	log (lȯg)	rat	rut	sod
fat	has (haz)	lop	red	sad	son (sən)
fed	her (hər)	lot	rib	sag	sop
fen	his (hiz)	lug	rid	Sal	sub
fib	if	nor (nȯr)	rig	Sam	sun
fig	is (iz)	of (ov)	rim	sap	sum
fin	lad	off (ȯf)	rip	sat	sup
fit	lag	or (ȯr)	rob	set	us
fog	lap	pal	rod	Sid	was (wäz)
fop	led				

ENDING IN *ff*	ENDING IN *ar*	ENDING IN *rr*	ENDING IN *ss*	ENDING IN *ll*
buff	bar (bär)	err (ər)	bass	all (ȯl)
cuff	car	burr (bər)	mass	ball
duff	far	purr (pər)	pass	call
huff	jar		Bess	bell
muff	mar		less	dell
puff	par		mess	fell
riff-raff	tar		hiss	Bill
ruff	war (wȯr)		miss	dill
			joss	fill
			boss (bȯs)	dull
			moss (mȯs)	gull
			toss (tȯs)	hull
			muss	bull (bu̇l)
				full (fu̇l)
				pull (pu̇l)

The Letters K and Q

In the letters *k* and *q*, the consonant blends *nk* and *sk*, and the speech consonant *ck*, the pupil meets new phonic problems. The pupil needs to learn that certain sounds can be written in two ways. The much more common hard *c* and the *k* have the same sound. If the child remembers that the *k* sounds like all the *c* sounds he has met thus far, he should have little difficulty pronouncing the words correctly.

The letter *k* does not occur too frequently at the beginning of the word. In this position it is more commonly the letter *c*. However, the *k* is much more frequent than the *c* at the end of the word. This knowledge should be especially helpful in spelling.

The letter *q* occurs only in the combination *qu* and usually has the sound of *kw*. It also may have the simple *k* sound as in *liquor*. Occasionally, the *kw* sound is separated as in *liquid* (lik'wid). *Que* at the end of a word is simply a *k* sound: *unique, clique, critique.**

Table IV lists some common monosyllabic words illustrating the *k, ck, nk, sk,* and the *qu* sounds.

TABLE IV

Monosyllabic Words Formed with K and Q and the Previously Learned Consonants and Vowels

ark	crock	hulk	knock	plunk	silk	stack
ask	dark	husk	knoll*	prank	skid	stalk*
back	deck	ilk	knot	prick	skiff	stark
balk*	Dick	ink	lack	punk	skill	stick
bank	disk	junk	lark	quack	skim	stink
bark	drank	keg	lock	quaff	skin	stock
bask	drink	kept	luck	quart*	skip	stuck
beck	duck	kick	mark	quell	skit	stunk
black	dunk	kid	mask	quest	skulk	sulk
blank	dusk	kill	milk	quick	skull	swank
blink	elk	kiln*	mink	quill	skunk	tack
brink	flank	kilt	monk	quilt	slack	talk*
brisk	flask	kin	muck	quit	slick	tank
buck	flunk	king	musk	rack	slink	task
bulk	folk*	kink	nick	rink	smock	tick
calk*	frank	kiss	Nick	risk	snack	trek
cask	Frank	kit	park	rock	sock	trick
click	frisk	knack	peck	sack	spank	walk*
clink	hack	knell	pick	sank	speck	wick
cluck	hock	knit	plank	sick	spunk	wink
crick	honk	knob	pluck			

---

* balk, (bȯk); calk (kȯk); folk (fōk); kiln (kil, kiln); knoll (nōl); stalk (stȯk); talk (tȯk); walk (wȯk); quart (kwȯrt).

An analysis of these words shows that most of them are phonetically consistent. The following observations, however, are in order.

1. The speech consonant *ck*, at the end of the word, preceded by a short vowel, is simply *k* as, for example, in *back, click, cluck, crick, crock, deck, Dick, duck, hack, hock, lack, lock, luck, nick, peck, pick, pluck, prick, rock, sack, sick, slack, slick, snack, sock, speck, stick.* Bailey[3] found this rule had 100 per cent validity.

2. *Ank* is *angk* as in *bank, blank, drank, flank, frank, plank, prank, sank, spank, swank, tank.*

3. *Ink* is *ingk* as in *kink, blink, brink, clink, drink, ink, pink, mink, rink, stink.*

4. *Unk* is *ǝngk* as in *bunk, dunk, flunk, junk, plunk, punk, skunk, spunk, stunk.*

5. *Onk* is *ängk* as in *honk*, or *ǝngk* as in *monk.*

6. *Kn* is simply an *n* as in *knack, knell, knit, knock, knob, knoll,* and *knot. GN* is simply *n* as in *gnash, gnat, gnaw.*

7. *Iss* is *is* as in *kiss; iff* is *if* as in *skiff; ill* is *il* as in *skill; aff* is *af* as in *quaff; ell* is *el* as in *quell.*

8. *A* when followed by *r* as in *ark, bark, dark, lark, mark, park, stark, quart* is the *ä* sound.

The Letters V, X, Y, Z

The four letters *v, x, y, z* commonly are the most difficult for the child to learn. The letter *x* spells six different sounds. Generally, it is either the *ks* or the *gz* sounds.

The consonant *y* is a palatal semivowel corresponding to the German *j* sound. It occurs only before vowels.

The letter *z* has two pronunciations: *z* and *zh*. The *y* has only one sound.

The pupil must become familiar with the sounds represented by these letters by familiarizing himself with words that contain them. The following lists of words illustrate the various sounds:

v sound: brave, breve, cave, clove, cove, crave, curve, dive, dove, drive, drove, Eve, eve, five, gave, give, grave, have, heave, hive, hives, jive, knave, live, love, move, pave, peeve, prove, rave, rove, save, salve, selves, sleeve, solve, starve, stove, vail, vain, vale, value, van, vane, vase, vast, vat, veal, veer, veil, vein, vend, vent, verb, vest, vet, vix, vie, view, vile, vim, vine, vise; vogue, voice, void, volt, vote, vouch, waive, wave, wives, wove.

ks sound of *x*: ax, box, coax, fix, fox, flax, flex, flux, hex, hoax, jinx, lax, Max, mix, next, ox, pix, pox, pyx, Rex, sex, six, tax, text, vex, wax.

y sound: yacht, yak, yams, yank, yap, yard, yarn, yawn, year, yea, yearn, yeast, yegg, yell, yelp, yen, yes, yet, yield, yip, yoke, yolk, yond, you, young, your, youth, yowl, yule.

z sound: adz, blaze, breeze, bronze, buss, craze, daze, doze, faze, fez, fiss, freeze, frieze, froze, fuzz, gauze, gaze, glaze, graze, haze, jazz, phiz, prize, quiz, raze, razz, size, sneeze, snooze, squeeze, waltz, wheeze, zeal, zest, zinc, zing, zip, zone, zoo, zoom.

The Soft Sounds of C and G

The pupil already has learned the hard sound of *c* and *g*. He also must become familiar with their soft sounds. *C* and *g* generally have a soft sound before *e, i,* or *y*;* *c* becomes an *s* as in *cede* and *g* becomes a *j* as in *age*. Emans[24] found that this generalization had a 90 per cent utility. In the exceptions, the *c* is pronounced *sh*. The most common exceptions to the *g* rule are *get, girl, give, tiger, finger*.

The soft sound at the end of a word usually is spelled *ce* (dance), *ge* (age), or *dge* (badge).** *Dge* occurs after short vowels; after a consonant the sound is spelled by *ge* (change). In words borrowed from the French (rouge, garage, mirage) *g* is a *zh* sound. The letter *c* also may have a *sh* sound, as in *vicious* or *ocean* or a *z* sound as in sacrifice and suffice. This occurs in words of more than one syllable.

Here are some common one-syllable words containing the soft *c* sound.

bounce	dunce	lace	place	splice
brace	face	lance	pounce	spruce
cede	farce	mice	prance	stance
cell	fence	mince	price	thence
cent	fierce	nice	prince	thrice
chance	fleece	niece	quince	trace
choice	flounce	once	race	trance
cinch	force	ounce	scarce	trice
cite	glance	pace	since	twice
cyst	grace	peace	slice	vice
dance	hence	pence	sluice	whence
deuce	ice	piece	source	wince
dice	juice	pierce	space	

Here are words illustrating the soft *g* sound.

age	doge	gibe	lodge	sludge
badge	dredge	gist	merge	smudge
barge	edge	gorge	nudge	splurge
bilge	flange	gourge	page	sponge

---

* When *c* is soft before *a*, it is written as *ç*.

** It may be desirable to introduce the pupil to the *gu* combination at this time. Examples are *guard, guess, guest, guide, guilt, guardhouse, guilty, guitar, intrigue, safeguard*. The *gu* in *penguin* is pronounced *gw*.

blunge	fledge	grange	pledge	stage
bridge	forge	grudge	plunge	stooge
budge	fringe	gurge	purge	strange
bulge	fudge	hedge	rage	surge
cage	gage	hinge	range	tinge
change	gauge	hodge-podge	ridge	trudge
charge	gem	huge	sage	urge
cringe	gene	judge	siege	verge
dirge	gent	large	sledge	wage
dodge	germ	liege		

The pupil might benefit in the learning of these words if they are grouped as follows:

bounce	mince	change
flounce	prince	grange
ounce	since	range
pounce	wince	strange

chance	barge	dredge
dance	charge	edge
glance	large	fledge
lance		hedge
prance		pledge
stance	budge	wedge
trance	fudge	
	grudge	
	judge	
fence	nudge	gurge
hence	sludge	purge
pence	smudge	splurge
thence	trudge	surge
whence		urge

Exercises for teaching the sounds of these letters may include the following:
1. Ask the pupil to say the names of the pictures below. Does the name begin with a hard or a soft sound? Draw a circle around the correct answer.

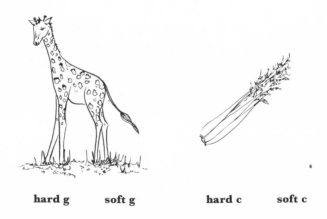

hard g   soft g   hard c   soft c

2. The pupil may be shown a series of words illustrating both the hard and the soft sound.

cat	cell
call	cent
can	circle
cut	cycle
cold	cyst
cure	nice

The pupil next is shown that in the above words, *c* is hard before the vowels *a*, *o*, and *u* and soft before the vowels *e*, *i*, and *y*.

3. The pupil is asked to make a rule for the *c* and/or *g* sound by filling in the blank spaces in a statement like the following: *c* usually has the soft sound when followed by the vowels, _____, _____, and _____, and it has the hard sound when followed by the vowels _____, _____, and _____.

4. The pupil must be taught the exceptions to the rule: get, girl, give.

Summary

This chapter concerned itself with the teaching of the beginning consonant. It is one of the first phonic skills that the pupil uses in reading. The chapter covered (1) the development of auditory, visual, and kinesthetic discrimination of the consonant sound, (2) the use of workbook and teacher-prepared materials to teach the consonant sounds, and (3) the special problems presented in the learning and teaching of each of the sounds.

Learning to handle beginning consonants is the first step in the development of a coding system. By seeing, hearing, and generally experiencing the sound and symbolization of consonants in total words, the pupil should develop a sense of word structure. It is the knowledge of word structure that permits the pupil to develop a coding system that will have applicability in many other word contexts. By seeing *b* function in numerous words as the sound he hears in *book*, the pupil gradually comes to expect that the *b* in a given instance will sound as the *b* in *book*. At any rate, it is the best guess that he can make.

The fact that the pupil will actually develop a coding system and that the coding system is developed by and through the experiencing of numerous words with only minimal spelling differences (cat, bat) is experientially validated. Children learn, for illustration, quite on their own such coding systems as "past tense ends in *ed*" (and say *selled* for *sold*) or that "the plural is formed by adding *s*" (and say *mans* for *men*).

IV

TEACHING THE SHORT-VOWEL SOUNDS

CHILDREN early learn to articulate both the short and the long vowel sounds. The short vowels are usually introduced before the long vowels because they occur most frequently in monosyllabic words, are phonetically more consistent, and occur more frequently in words that the pupil meets in initial reading. The most natural sequence in learning the vowel sounds seems to be (1) learning the meaning of vowel, (2) learning the short-vowel sounds, (3) learning the long-vowel sounds, (4) learning to discriminate between the short and long vowel, (5) learning the effect of adding an *e* to a syllable containing a short vowel in the medial position, and (6) learning the sound of two vowels written together.

Teaching vowel sounds is difficult because there is such great variability in the sounds that vowels or vowel combinations may have. Appendix III illustrates these variations. Beginning phonic instruction should avoid these variations. It is recommended that the teacher begin with the short-vowel sound.

Steps in Teaching Short-Vowel Sounds

The teaching procedure outlined in this chapter assumes that the pupil has learned what the vowels are and that they have at least two sounds. After this has been learned, teaching of the short vowel may proceed through the following steps:

1. The teacher pronounces some words that contain the short *a* sound such as *bat, fat, cat, rat, cap, sat, Ann, at, am, and, apple*. The *a* sound may be slightly elongated. This teaches the pupil to listen for the short-vowel sound. The teacher may identify each sound with a jingle such as the following:

A a*	*E e**
Apple, apple	Egg, egg,
Come to me	I like it best.
From the big,	The hen will lay one
Tall apple tree	In her nest.

---

* Reprinted by permission from *Time for Phonics, Book A* by Louise Binder Scott. Copyright © 1962 by McGraw-Hill, Inc.

2. The teacher asks the pupils what they noticed about the middle sound in the words that he gave: *cap, bat, cat.* Were the middle sounds alike or different?

3. The teacher then may pronounce words, some of which contain the short-vowel sound and some of which do not. The pupils raise their hands when the word contains the short *a* sound.

4. The pupils pronounce the words and are asked to give other words containing the short *a* sound. The teacher may ask if there is anyone in the the class whose name contains a short *a* sound.

5. The pupil is taught that the sound he has been hearing in the words given by the teacher is the short *a* sound.

6. The teacher prints the letter *a* on the blackboard and writes out words such as *at, am, bat, mat, pat, hat.* He underlines the short *a* sound and notes that in each instance one consonant follows the vowel. The pupil is told that there are five vowels, *a, e, i, o, u,* and that each of these has a long and a short sound. "Today we are learning the short *a* sound." The teacher may give a key picture for each of the vowel sounds. For *a,* it might be an apple; for *e,* an egg or an elephant; for *i,* an Indian or ink; *o,* an ox or an ostrich; and for *u,* an umbrella. The teacher may associate the short *a* with an apple and may call it the "apple sound." The teacher may post different pictures on the blackboard and may ask the pupils to draw a line under any pictures whose names contain a short *a* sound.

7. The teacher then writes a name under each picture whose name contains a short *a* sound. He underlines the short *a* and notes that it is called the short *a* sound. He again sounds the words, moving his finger across the word from left to right, and makes sure that the pupils listen carefully to the sound in the middle of the word. He gives the short *a* sound a slight emphasis.

8. The pupils say the words in unison or individually.

9. The pupils next are taught to associate the short *a* sound with both the capital and the lowercase letter. They may be shown that a word like *apple* may be written with a small *a* or a capital *A.*

10. The pupils next print the letter *a,* both the capital and the lowercase.

Workbooks and other teacher-prepared materials may then be used to teach the sounds. The following exercises are illustrative:

1. Look at the pictures below. Note that each has the short *e* sound as in *egg,* and that it is followed by a consonant.

net   **hen**   **pen**

2. Put a line through each picture that has a short *a* sound in the middle.

3. Write the missing vowel.

$$\underline{h\ \_\ t} \qquad\qquad \underline{c\ \_\ t}$$

    x   x

4. Draw a line from the letter *e* to the pictures whose names have the same sound.

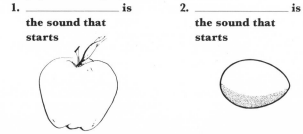

Ee

As soon as the pupil has mastered more than one vowel, exercises such as the following are helpful.

1. Have the pupil write the proper vowel on the line.

1. _____ is   2. _____ is
    the sound that   **the sound that**
    starts   **starts**

2. Have the pupil circle the word that rhymes with the name of the picture and let him write the word.

bat _____   ham _____   pan _____
man _____   map _____   tap _____

3. Have the pupil write the missing vowel.

4. Have the pupil circle the vowel sound that he hears.

5. Make a circular card similar to the one below. Write the beginning and ending consonant on the card and put the short vowels on a strip of paper. The pupil pulls the strip of paper through the opening revealing new words.

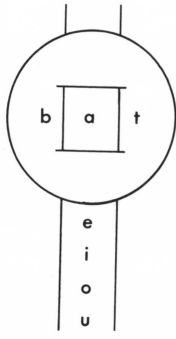

6. Have the pupil fill in the missing vowel in exercises such as the following:

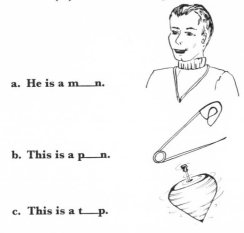

a. He is a m___n.

b. This is a p___n.

c. This is a t___p.

Through exercises like those above, the pupil needs to learn the following:

1. The letters, *a, e, i, o,* and *u,* are vowels.
2. When these letters say their names, they have a long sound.
3. These vowels also have a short sound. The short sounds of the five vowels are best illustrated in words like *a*pple, *e*gg, *i*nk, *o*x, and *u*mbrella.
4. The technique of medial-vowel substitution also must be taught. The pupil learns that changing the vowel alters both the appearance of the word and its meaning. The pupil must be taught medial-vowel substitution inductively. He must see what changing the vowel does to the form of the word, to its pronunciation, and to its meaning. The vocabulary suggested in Tables I and III provides numerous possibilities for teaching the skill; for example, *bat* may become *bet, bit, but; cat* may become *cot* or *cut; hat* may be changed to *hit, hot, hut;* and *pat* may become *pet, pit,* or *pot.*
5. When there is only one vowel in a word, that word is a one-syllable or monosyllabic word.
6. When there is only one vowel in a word (as in words like *at* and *bat*), and when that vowel is followed by a single consonant (a*t* or ba*t*), then the vowel is usually a short vowel. The pupil should study examples such as the following:

at		in	on	up
bat	hen	pin	top	nut

He next learns to apply his knowledge to new words.

7. The pupil learns to apply the rule, principle, or generalization to the accented syllable in polysyllabic words:

tiptop	bobbin	bandit	bellhop
bonnet	bigtop	bedbug	cabin

The *ä* Sound of *a*

Early in his phonic training the pupil needs to learn the *ä* sound of *a*. This is the sound which the pupil meets in such words as *bar* or *car*. The following vocabulary is helpful in teaching the sound.

bar	mar	bark	mark
car	par	dark	park
far	tar	hark	
jar		lark	

After the pupil has learned the consonant blends and the speech consonants, he should be able to identify such words as the following:

Clark	spar	star
scar	spark	

The Short *o* Sound of *a*

The *a* often has a short *o* sound. The following sounds illustrate this use.

swab	wand	watt	wallup	washroom
swamp	want	what	wanting	watchdog
swan	was	swallow	washing	watchful
swap	wash	tightwad	washrag	watchman
swat	wasp	waffle	washcloth	wattage
wad	watch	wallet	washer	whitewash

The *ò* Sound of *a*

The *ò* sound occurs when the *a* is followed by *ll*. The following words illustrate this use.

all	hall	wall	stall
ball	mall	small	squall
call	tall		

The *ô* Sound of *a*

Another sound of *a* that the pupil will meet early is that of *ô* which occurs in the following words:

dwarf	warm	walnut	warlike
swarm	warp	warble	warmly
war	wart	warden	warming
ward	walleye	wardrobe	warrant

The Short *u* Sound of *o*

Early in his phonic education the pupil must learn that the English language is not entirely alphabetic. There are exceptions. Perhaps, one of the first exceptions he will need to be able to handle is the short *u* sound of *o*. The following monosyllabic and polysyllabic words are illustrative of this short *u* sound of the letter *o*.

come	blossom	gallop	mongrel	salmon
does	boredom	galop	monkey	scaffold
done	bottom	godson	month	season
dove	button	govern	monthly	seldom
glove	cannon	grandson	mormon	sermon
love	carrot	hammock	mother	smother
none	canyon	handsome	mutton	shovel
one	color	havoc	oneself	stomach
shove	comfort	honey	oneway	scallop
some	coming	idol	oven	someone
son	common	income	parrot	sometime
ton	compass	kingdom	patron	sometimes
won	confront	lemon	phantom	someway
abbot	cotton	lesson	pilot	summon
above	cover	lonesome	pivot	symbol
among	crayon	loveless	piston	symptom
apron	donkey	lovely	poison	synod
atom	dragon	loving	prison	tendon
bacon	dozen	mammon	purpose	tiresome
ballot	falcon	mammoth	random	wagon
baron	felon	matron	ransom	welcome
beacon	flagon	melon	reason	wisdom
become	freedom	method	reckon	zealot
bigot	frontal	Monday	ribbon	
bishop	gallon	money	riot	

It is interesting to note that in most instances the *o* is followed by *m, n, p, t,* or *v*.

An exercise such as the following teaches the pupil to discriminate between the short *o* and the short *u* sound of *o*. Have the pupil circle the correct pronunciation.

a. A ton $\left[\begin{array}{c} \text{tun} \\ \text{ton} \end{array}\right]$ of gold.

b. A lot $\left[\begin{array}{c} \text{lot} \\ \text{lut} \end{array}\right]$ of fish.

c. A son $\left[\begin{array}{c} \text{sun} \\ \text{son} \end{array}\right]$ of Jim.

d. He has done $\left[\begin{array}{c} \text{dun} \\ \text{don} \end{array}\right]$ his job.

The Schwa

An analysis of two-syllable words reveals that the letter preceding the final letter is a word often is silent when followed by *n* or *l*.

bison	garden	lesson	metal	prison
bitten	glisten	lighten	model	redden
button	glutton	listen	mitten	rotten
chosen	gotten	madden	mutton	sadden
christen	hasten	maiden	pardon	sharpen
cotton	hidden	mason	parson	sudden
dozen	kitten	mantel	petal	tassel
frozen	lessen	medal	pistol	tighten
				widen

This softening of the vowel sound in unstressed syllables is often termed the schwa sound of the vowel and is represented by the symbol ə. The use of the schwa sound should be explained to the pupil when he begins to use the dictionary.

Summary

Chapter IV summarized some of the problems as well as the techniques to be used in the teaching of the short-vowel sounds. While vowels are not as alphabetically regular as are most consonants, there is sufficient consistency to warrant teaching of certain basics. The pupil should gradually be able to deal with the principle of position. This simply says that the sound of the vowel changes depending upon its position in the word.

After the pupil has mastered the sound of vowels in the beginning or medial position in monosyllabic words, he should be ready to deal with the short sound of the vowel in one-syllable words in which a single vowel beginning the word is followed by a single consonant, for example, *am, an, as, at, Ed, if, in, is, it, of, on, up, us*. The first vowel rule then may be stated thus: *A single vowel at the beginning or in the middle of a one syllable word usually is short*. Emans[24] found that this rule had 80 per cent utility.

V
TEACHING THE END CONSONANT SOUNDS

It would appear logical that after the pupil has learned to deal with the consonants in the beginning position and the short vowel in the beginning and medial position, he might learn to deal with the consonant in the end position.

Techniques for Teaching End Consonants

The techniques which were useful in teaching the beginning consonant can be used in teaching end-consonant substitution.

1. The teacher pronounces some words which end with the *t* sound such as *hat, but, net, nut.* The end sound may be slightly elongated or stressed, but it should not be distorted.
2. The teacher asks the pupils what they noticed about the end sound. Were the sounds alike or different?
3. The pupils are asked to give other words ending with a *t* sound.
4. The teacher pronounces words, some of which end with the *t* sound and some of which do not. The pupils raise their hands when the word ends with a *t* sound. The teacher may put pictures on the board and asks the pupils to name the picture. He then may ask the pupil to identify the pictures or words that have the same ending sound.

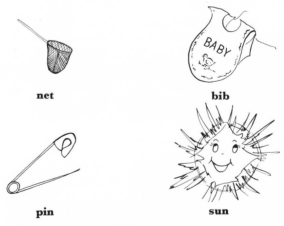

net   bib

pin   sun

5. The teacher prints the letter *t* on the blackboard and writes out the words *hat, but, net,* and *nut* or any other word ending with a *t* that the youngsters mentioned.

6. The pupils are told to look carefully at the letter ending each of the words. The teacher again sounds the words making sure that the pupils listen carefully to the sound at the end of each word.

7. The pupils read the words in unison.

8. The teacher shows the pupil that substituting one final consonant for another completely changes the word. The word *pet,* for example, may become *pen* or *pep*; *tan* may become *tap* or *tab*. The pupil must learn that changing of the final consonant both alters the word and falsifies the meaning. In the sentence "Bob wants a pet," changing the *t* on pe*t* to an *n* alters the meaning of the utterance. At this stage the pupil is learning consonant substitution.

Workbooks and other teacher-prepared materials may then be used to teach the end sounds. Teaching of phonograms, rhyming, and of end consonants is very similar.

The following exercises are illustrative:

1. Have the pupil check whether the names of a series of pictures end like a given key word.

Ending

t   **hat**

Does the word end like hat?

yes no   yes no

yes no   yes no

2. Have pupils pick from a series of letters the one that completes a word. Write the end consonant.

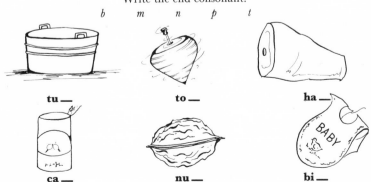

b   *m*   *n*   *p*   *t*

tu __   to __   ha __

ca __   nu __   bi __

3. Have pupils write the proper consonant in the blank space. In this exercise the letters are not listed as in exercise two.

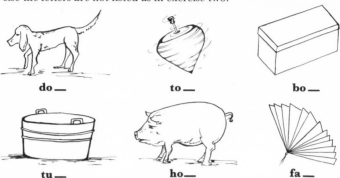

do __   to __   bo __

tu __   ho __   fa __

4. Have the pupils note whether a given letter occurs first or last in a word.
Is the letter sound above the picture first or last in the word?
Circle the correct answer.

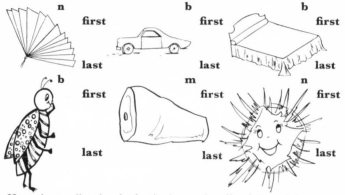

n
first
last

b
first
last

b
first
last

b
first
last

m
first
last

n
first
last

5. Have the pupil write the beginning and ending letter of the name of a picture.
What letters come before and after the vowel?

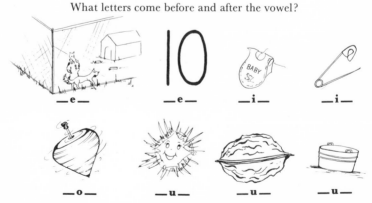

__ e __   __ e __   __ i __   __ i __

__ o __   __ u __   __ u __   __ u __

6. Have the pupil complete exercises like the following by writing the beginning and end consonant in the blank spaces.

a. Ben has a pet __

b. The pup bit the __

7. Have the pupil select the correct consonant ending:

a. Tom has a pet pu t. / p.

b. Pam has a pet cu p. / b.

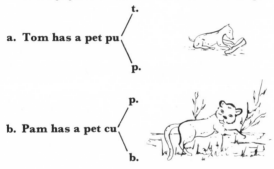

The Phonogram

One of the basic sound-sense patterns in the language is the phonogram.* Some even suggest that the phonogram is *the* natural unit of the English language. The phonogram is a closed syllable which begins with a vowel (*eg, eb, ac, in, ill, ate, ing, oat*), and which produces a single speech sound. The phonogram is generally phonetically stable and regular in sounding, its form is consistent, and it has a basic utility in reading.

Joos[34] notes that the sounding of vowels is regulated (in most cases) by the letter pattern which follows the vowel and that since

---

* The phonogram method was developed by Virginia W. Jones, George T. Gabriel, and Loyal W. Joos, and is presented in *The Phonogram Method: A New Approach to First Grade Reading*. Materials are available through Virginia Jones, State University College, Oswego, New York.

the phonogram has the vowel plus its following letter pattern, the reader soon learns to see the entire pattern as a unit. Experience indicates that this is exactly what happens. Pupils taught to analyze words into phonograms quickly read sound-symbol patterns and are not limited by letter-by-letter perception.

Joos writes:

> . . . the stability of the phonogram eliminates much of the tedious teaching of rules. For example, if *ite, ate, ike, oat, ain, air* et cetera are taught as graphemes demanding an immediate oral response, the deductive teaching of vowel rules can be postponed until a later date when such teaching will not "slow up" the beginner's progress. Of course, I would advocate teaching only one phoneme per grapheme at first (*green, seen, queen*, not *been*).

A student of reading quickly recognizes the similarity between the phonogram method and the "word family" approach. The phonogram method, however, is different in two ways:

1. Spacing is the key to the utilization of grapheme-phoneme correspondence that is natural in the flow of the language. Usually two and never more than four words containing the same phonogram should be introduced in any one passage.
2. Pupils learning phonogram analysis are moved as quickly as possible from monosyllabic words to words containing more than one syllable. Thus pupils learn that *an* is a stable unit whether it occurs in initial, medial, or lateral positions; initial —*an*imal; medial—adv*an*cing; and lateral—r*an*.

By the time the pupil has mastered the beginning and end consonants and short vowels, he should be able to deal with the following phonograms.*

ab	eb	ib	ob	ub
ac	ed	ic	od	ud
ad	eg	id	og	uff
aff	ell	if	om	ug
ag	em	iff	on	ull (dull)
am	en	ig	op	um
an	ep	ill	ot	un
ap	ess	im	ox	up
as	et	in		us
at	ex	ip		ut
ax		is		
		iss		
		it		
		ix		

---

* Schmitt, Hall and McCreary Company, Minneapolis, offers two sets of cards in booklet form which illustrate various phonograms and phonogram families.

In addition, he probably will have learned such common endings as *all, ar, off, oll, oss,* and *alk.* Here are some other phonograms that the pupil might profitably learn in the elementary years.

and	ee	ike	oke	ove	unk
ake	eet	ing	ook	old	uy
ay	eep	ine	own	ood	ure
ack	ent	ight	oy	ough	ush
ank	ead	ich	ouse	oil	
arne	ease	ilk	ome	onk	
arn	eat	ith	ool	ought	
alk	ern	ird	ow	orn	
arm	eak	ink	oom	oast	
aid	een	ick	oot	ound	
age	eel	ile	ore		
atch	eek	int	orse		
	each	igh	out		
		itch	our		

The Double Consonant Ending

The pupil will soon meet words which double the final consonant, but in which only one of the consonants is pronounced. This doubling of the final consonant is common with *f, l,* and *s.* The pupil's problem tends to be more of a spelling problem than a reading problem. Here is a list of words useful in teaching the words.

ENDING IN *ff*	ENDING IN *ss*	ENDING IN *ll*		
buff	bass	all (ôl)	Nell	sill
cuff	mass	ball	sell	till
duff	pass	call	tell	will
huff	Bess	fall	well	cull
Jeff	less	gall	yell	dull
muff	mess	hall	Bill	gull
off	hiss	pall	dill	hull
puff	miss	tall	fill	lull
riff-raff	joss	wall	hill	mull
ruff	boss (bòs)	bell	ill	null
	moss (mòs)	fell	Jill	bull (bùl)
	toss (tòs)	hell	mill	full (fùl)
	cuss	jell	pill	pull (pùl)
	muss	mell	rill	

The most common exceptions are *if, of, clef, as, was, gas, has, yes, is, his, this, us, bus, pus.* After the pupil can handle consonant blends the following words should be learned: *dwell; bliss, bless, brass, class, cross, dress, glass, grass; bluff, cliff, skiff, sniff.*

A workbook exercise helpful in teaching the doubling of the final consonant may require the pupil to underline the correct form in sentences such as the following:

a. The hen got (of, off) the top of the hut.
b. Jeff has a can (of, off) pop.
c. Dad is filling his car with (gas, gass).
d. The cat (hised, hissed) at the dog.

Summary

By the time the pupil has attained the stage of phonic development described in this chapter he should have developed a coding system that helps him to "read through" thousands of words.

VI

CONSONANT BLENDS AND
SPEECH CONSONANTS

THIS chapter is concerned chiefly with two and three letter combinations of consonants. These are usually labeled *consonant blends* and *speech consonants*.

Consonant Blends

The consonant blends must be distinguished from the speech consonants, *ch, sh, th, wh, ck, gh, ph, qu,* and *ng.* These latter are digraphs and thus are two consonants that have a single speech sound. The consonant blends, on the other hand, consist of two or more letters each having its own distinct sound. The following consonant blends occur: *bl, br, chr, cl, cr, dr, dw, fl, fr, gl, gr, nk, pl, pr, sc, scr, shr, sk, sl, sm, sn, sp, sq, spl, spr, sch, st, str, thr, tr,* and *tw.* Of all the double consonants, only *st, sp,* and *sk* occur both at the beginning and at the end of a word.

The order in which to introduce the consonant blends is somewhat arbitrary. Three-letter blends should be introduced after two-letter blends. Fry[26] has grouped the blends in terms of frequency of use: *st, pr, tr, gr, br, pl, sp, cr, cl, dr, fr, sc, bl, fl, sk, sl, sw, sm, gl, sn, tw.* It may also be desirable to group the blends in families: *br, cr, dr, fr, gr, pr; bl, cl, fl, gl, pl, sl; sc, sk, sm, sn, sp, st, sw; scr, str, spr, shr, spl, sch.*

Here is a list of words that we have found helpful in teaching each of the blends. Many of these words can be illustrated pictorially.

bl: blot, blanket, blade, blotter, black, block, blue, blob, blink, blank, blacktop, blame, bless, bliss, bluff, blink, bled, blaze.

br: brad, brag, bran, brass, brat, bred, brim, bring, broom, bracelet, branch, bridle, briefcase, bridegroom, bride, bread, bridge, brick, brown, broomstick, bracket, brute, brink, brisk, broke, brave, brace.

cl: clad, clam, clan, clap, class, clef, cliff, cling, clip, clod, clog, clot, club, clown, cloud, clock, claw, classroom, clamp, clove, click, cluck, clink, close.

cr: crayon, cracker, croquet, crowbar, cross, crown, crate, crack, crock, crane, crime, cry, crave, craze.

dr: dress, drumstick, drink, drawer, dragon, dresser, dryer, drape, drugstore, druggist, drank, drunk, dry, drive.

dw: dwarf, dwell, dwelling.

fl: flapjack, flagpole, flashlight, flower, fly, flake, fling, flame, fluke, flank, flask, flunk.

fr: freighter, friar, frame, fruit, Frank, frisk, fry, froze.

gl: globe, glove, glasses, glare.

gr: grapefruit, grandstand, griddle, grave, grape, green, gray, grasshopper, grime, gripe, grade, graze, grace, grass.

pl: plate, plume, planter, pliers, plow, plane, plank, plant, pluck, ply, place.

pr: pretzel, prune, present, propellor, protractor, priest, prime, probe, prove, prose, prank, pry, prize, price.

sc: scooter, scale, scarf, scarecrow, scare, scope.

sk: skate, skull, skeleton, skunk, ski, skillet, skirt, sky, skid, skiff, skim, skin, skit.

sl: slide, slack, slate, slime, slope, slick, sly, slice.

sm: smack, smoke, smock, smile, smite.

sn: snake, snowman, snack, snowshoes, snail, snare, snore.

sp: spade, spy, spank, spark plug, sparrow, spider, spoon, spool, sparkle, spare, spire, spike, spine, speck, spunk, space.

sq: squat, squall, squid, squint.

st: stagecoach, starfish, stoplight, steamboat, stop sign, steeple, stove, stick, stool, stairs, stake, stable, stapler, statue, store, stunk, stuck, stock, stink, sty, stack, stale, stare, stoke, stole, stone.

sw: swing, sweater, swallow, swan, sweat shirt, switch, sweeper.

tr: train, truck, tree, tractor, trick, track, triangle, trunk, tray, trinket, tricycle, trophy, tramp, trailer, tripod, trash, trade, tribe, try, trace.

tw: twenty, twelve, tweezers, twinkle, twins, twine, twice.

Since the early phonic experiences emphasized primarily the short vowel sounds, the pupil should have little difficulty pronouncing the following phonograms:

a: *ab, ac, ad, aff, ag, all, am, an, ap, ar, ass, at*

e: *eb, ec, ed, eff, eg, ell, em, en, ep, ess, et*

i: *ib, ic, id, iff, ig, ill, im, in, ip, iss, is*

o: *ob, oc, od, og, om on, op, ot*

u: *ub, uc, ud, uff, ug, ull, um, un, up, uss, ut*

Most of these syllables he has pronounced as parts of words. He also has learned to make initial consonant substitution. He has learned that by changing the initial consonant he can change *cab* to *dab*, *gab*, or *nab*.

Now he must extend this process. Instead of substituting one consonant for another, he substitutes two consonants for one. Thus *cab* becomes *crab*, *grab*, *scab*, *slab*, or *stab*.

Teaching the initial consonant blend begins with the same procedure as the teaching of the beginning consonant. This was outlined in Chapter III, and you may want to refer to pages 38–40.

After the pupil has developed an auditory, visual, and kinesthetic discrimination of the sound in the total context of the word, workbook and other teacher-prepared materials may then be used to continue the teaching of consonant blends and the technique of consonant substitution. The following exercises are illustrative. For additional ones, see the chapter on teaching beginning consonants.

1. Have the pupils look at the pictures below. Say the name of each picture. Note that each begins like the key word *broom*.

bread   **bridge**   **brush**

2. Have the pupil put a line through the two pictures in each row that begin with the same sound.

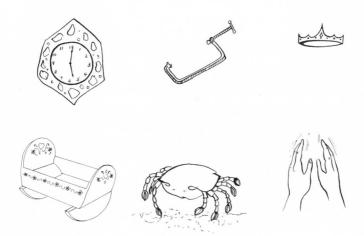

3. Have pupils circle each word that begins like the name of the picture.

drink   clip   crab   drip

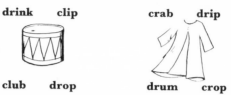

club   drop   drum   crop

4. Have the pupils write or circle the proper consonant blend in various types of exercises.

   a. Have the pupil circle the correct beginning letter sound.

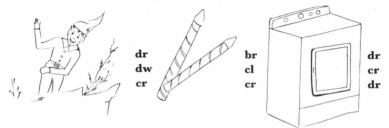

dr	**br**		**dr**
dw	**cl**		**cr**
cr	**cr**		**dr**

   b. Have the pupil write under each picture the initial consonant blend of the name of each picture.

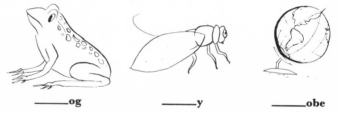

———og   ——y   ———obe

5. Have the pupil circle the word that gives meaning to the sentence and that agrees with the picture at the end of the line.

a. This is a < **crab.**
                   crib.

b. Peg's doll is in a < **crib.**
                          crab.

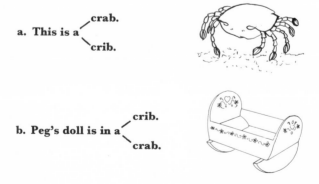

6. Have the pupil fill in the blank in the sentence with one of the letters at the end of the sentence, thus giving meaning to the sentence.

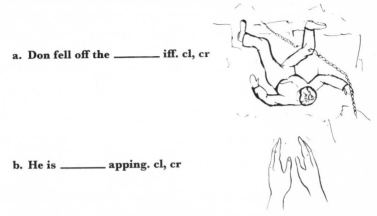

a. Don fell off the _____ iff. cl, cr

b. He is _____ apping. cl, cr

7. A phonic wheel similar to the one illustrated in DeBoer and Dallmann[18] is useful in providing drill with the consonant blends. The wheel is made of two circles of tagboard. One circle is slightly smaller than the other and contains a smaller indentation. It is fastened at the center upon the larger circle. As the pupil turns the top circle, he meets various words beginning with the consonant blend to be studied.

The pupil also needs to learn to deal with the three-letter blends: *chr, sch, scr, shr, spl, spr, str, thr*. Here are common monosyllable words beginning with these combinations:

chr :   Christ, chrome
sch :   scheme, school
scr :   screech, screen, scroll, script, scrunch
shr :   shrank, shred, shrewd, shriek, shrill, shrimp, shrine, shrink, shroud, shrub, shrug
spl :   splash, spleen, splice, splint, split, splotch, splurge
spr :   sprain, sprang, sprawl, spray, spread, spree, spring, sprint, sprite, sprout, spruce, sprung, spray
str :   strafe, strain, strait, strand, strap, straw, stray, streak, stream, street, strength, stress, stretch, stride, strife, strike, string, stripe, strive, strode, stroll, strong, strove, stray, struck, strung
thr :   thrash, thread, threat, three, thresh, threw, thrice, thrift, thrill, throat, throb, throng, through, throw, thrush, thrust

The consonant trigraphs such as *chm* (drachm) and *ght* (thought), representing a single speech sound, should be taught after the pupil has mastered three-letter blends.

Teaching the Ending Consonant Blends

After the pupil has learned to handle some of the beginning consonant blends, he is ready to learn the end consonant blends. Table V contains a list of some common two-consonant endings.

The pupil cannot be expected to learn all of these at one time. How the teacher introduces them will depend on the vocabulary to which the pupil can react with meaning.

TABLE V

COMMON DOUBLE-CONSONANT WORD ENDINGS

act (akt)	elf (elf)	off (óf)
aff (baff—baf)	ell (fell—fel)	oft (óft)
aft (raft—raft)	elm (elm)	old (ōld)
alb (alb)	elp (help—help)	olf (wolf—wůlf)
alc (talc—talk)	elt (belt—belt)	olm (holm—hōm)
ald (bald—bōld)	emp (hemp)	olt (bolt—bōlt)
alf (calf—kaf)	end (end)	omb (bomb—bäm)
all (ól)	ens (lens—lenz)	omb (tomb—tüm)
alm (balm—bäm)	ent (lent—lent)	omp (romp—rämp)
alp (alp)	ept (wept—wept)	ond (fond—fänd)
alt (halt—hólt)	erd (herd—hərd)	ong (long—lóng)
amb (lamb—lam)	erg (berg—bərg)	ont (font—fänt)
amp (tamp—tamp)	erm (term—tərm)	orb (órb)
amp (swamp—swämp)	ern (fern—fərn)	ord (ford—fōrd)
and (and)	ert (ert—pərt)	orm (form—fōrm)
ang (bang)	est (pest—pest)	orn (horn—hórn)
anns (banns—banz)	iff (stiff—stif)	ort (fort—fōrt)
ant (ant)	ift (lift—lift)	oss (toss—tós)
apt (apt)	ild (wild—wīld)	ost (lost—lóst)
arb (garb—gärb)	ilm (film—film)	uct (duct—dəkt)
arc (ärk)	ilt (hilt—hilt)	ull (dull—dəll)
ard (lard—lärd)	imb (climb—klīm)	ull (pull—půl)
arf (scarf—skärf)	imp (limp—limp)	ulp (gulp—gəlp)
arl (marl—märl)	ind (bind—bīnd)	ult (cult-kəlt)
arm (ärm)	ing (sing—sing)	umb (dumb—dəm)
arn (barn—bärn)	inn (in)	ump (dump—dəmp)
arp (carp—kärp)	int (lint—lint)	und (fund—fənd)
arr (parr—pär)	ird (bird—bərd)	ung (lung—ləng)
art (ärt)	irl (girl—gərl)	unt (bunt—bənt)
asm (chasm—kaz'm)	irm (firm—fərm)	urb (curb—kərb)
asp (asp)	irn (firn—firn)	urd (curd—kərd)
ass (ass)	irt (girt—gərt)	urf (surf—sərf)
ast (last—last)	isc (disc—disk)	urg (burg—bərg)
att (batt—bat)	ism (iz'm)	url (hurl—hərl)
ebs (plebs—plebz)	isp (lisp—lisp)	urn (burn—bərn)
ecs (specs—speks)	iss (miss—mis)	urp (burp—bərp)
ect (sect—sekt)	ist (list—list)	urt (hurt—hərt)
eft (left—left)	itt (mitt)	ust (just—jəst)
eld (held—held)		utt (mutt—mət)

Exercises such as the following will be useful in teaching the end consonant blends:

1. Have the pupil check whether the name of a series of pictures ends like a given key word.

*c*k   **du***ck*

Does the word end like duck?

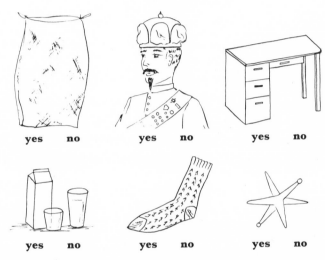

yes   no   **yes   no**   **yes   no**

yes   no   **yes   no**   **yes   no**

2. Have pupils pick from a series of consonant blends the one that completes the name of a picture.

ck,   nk,   ff,   lb,   ll

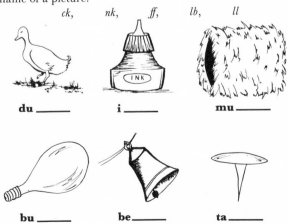

du _____   **i** _____   **mu** _____

bu _____   **be** _____   **ta** _____

3. Have pupils complete the spelling of each word by adding *k* or *ck*.

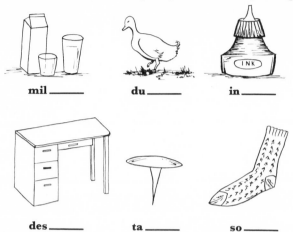

mil _____ **du** _____ **in** _____

des _____ **ta** _____ **so** _____

Another variant of this exercise requires the pupil simply to circle the correct ending.

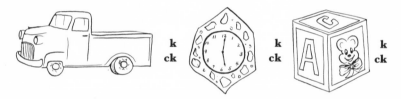

    k   **k**   **k**
    ck   **ck**   **ck**

4. Have the pupil complete exercises like the following by filling in the correct consonant ending:

a. This is a ca _____ .

b. This is a ba _____ .

c. Bob can ju _____.

d. This is a ha _____.

The following words are useful in teaching the end consonants:

ck: back, hack, jack, lack, Mack, pack, quack, rack, sack, tack, black, crack, slack, smack, snack, stack, track, deck, heck, neck, peck, Dick, kick, lick, Mick, nick, Nick, pick, quick, sick, brick, click, flick, prick, slick, stick, trick, tick, wick, cock, dock, hock, lock, mock, rock, sock, tock, block clock, crock, flock, frock, smock, buck, duck, luck, suck, tuck, cluck, pluck, stuck, truck.

ct: act, pact, tact, fact, duct, sect, tract, Pict, strict.

ff: staff, chaff, gaff, quaff, cliff, miff, skiff, sniff, stiff, tiff, whiff, doff, scoff, off, bluff, buff, cuff, fluff, gruff, huff, luff, muff, puff, scuff, snuff, stuff, tuff.

ft: raft, draft, craft, graft, shaft, aft, left, cleft, theft, lift, drift, swift, gift, shift, thrift, sift, croft, loft, oft, soft, tuft.

lb: bulb.

ld: bald, scald, held, weld, bold, cold, fold, gold, hold, mold, old, sold, told.

lf: calf, half, elf, self, shelf, golf, wolf.

ll: all, ball, call, fall, gall, hall, pall, small, squall, stall, tall, wall, bell, cell, dell, dwell, ell, fell, sell, shell, smell, spell, swell, tell, well, yell, bill, brill, chill, dill, drill, fill, frill, gill, grill, hill, ill, kill, mill, pill, quill, rill, shrill, sill, skill, spill, still, thrill, will, doll, bull, full, pull, cull, dull, gull, hull, skull.

lm: balm, calm, psalm, palm, elm, whelm, helm, realm.

lp: alp, scalp, help, yelp, gulp, pulp.

lt: fault, halt, malt, salt, vault, exalt, belt, dealt, dwelt, felt, knelt, melt, pelt, welt, built, guilt, hilt, jilt, kilt, lilt, tilt, wilt, bolt, colt, holt, jolt, molt, cult, adult.

mb: lamb, bomb, tomb, dumb, numb.

mp: pump, stamp, tramp, clamp, ramp, blimp, camp, hump, stump, clump, dump, cramp, damp, lamp, tamp, limp, romp, pomp, stomp, bump, lump, plump, rump, slump, trump, damp.

nd: band, bland, brand, gland, grand, hand, land, sand, stand, wand, bend, end, blend, lend, mend, rend, send, spend, tend, trend, wend, wind, bond, fond, blond, pond, fund.

ng: bang, fang, gang, hang, pang, rang, sang, slang, tang, bing, ding, king, wing, ping, ring, sing, sling, sting, swing, ting, bong, dong, gong, long, song, pong, tong, rung, slung, stung, sung, swung.

nk: bank, sank, tank, blank, clank, crank, drank, flank, frank, plank, prank, spank, tank, fink, kink, link, mink, pink, sink, wink, blink, brink, drink, slink, stink, honk, bunk, dunk, junk, punk, sunk, drunk, flunk, skunk, spunk, stunk, trunk.

ens: lens.

nt: ant, can't, grant, pant, plant, rant, scant, slant, want, bent, dent, lent, sent, spent, tent, went, lint, dint, flint, glint, hint, mint, print, stint, tint, font, front, blunt, brunt, bunt, grunt, hunt, punt, runt, stunt.

pt: apt, rapt, kept, slept, swept, wept.

rb: garb, barb.

rd: lard, bard, card, hard, ward, yard, curd, lord, chord, cord.

rf: dwarf, wharf, serf, surf, turf.

rl: snarl, gnarl, Carl, earl, twirl, burl, churl, curl, furl, girl, hurl, knurl, pearl, purl, swirl, whirl, uncurl, unfurl.

rm: farm, harm, warm, alarm, charm, storm, form, worm, squirm, term.

rn: darn, warn, yearn, earn, learn, fern, urn, turn, concern.

rp: harp, carp, sharp, warp, slurp, burp, chirp.

rt: art, Art, cart, dart, part, smart, tart, wart, hurt, curt, dirt, shirt, pert, sort, court.

sc: disc.

sk: desk, disk, flask, cask, mask, ask, bask, task, tusk, dusk, frisk, brisk, husk, musk, risk.

sm: spasm, prism.

sp: clasp, asp, gasp, grasp, lisp, crisp, rasp, hasp, wisp, cusp.

ss: pass, miss, hiss, toss, bass.

st: nest, mast, fist, cast, mist, frost, crust, blast, last, dust, lost, test, best, rest, rust, pest, just, twist, bust, crest, gust, hast, blest, jest, west, trust.

tt: mitt.

The Speech Consonants

The speech consonants, as we stated at the beginning of the chapter, are *ch, sh, th, wh, ck, gh, ph, qu,* and *ng.* Here we are concerned only with *ch, sh, th, wh, gh, ph.* By the time the pupil comes to consider this content, he already has had experience with digraphs or with two letters having one sound, especially with *ck* and *qu.* Now we extend this principle to the speech consonants, *ch, sh, th, wh, gh,* and *ph.* Digraphs are not a blend of two letters; the sound is distinctive.

The Digraph *ch*

The digraph *ch* may have four distinct sounds: *ch, j, sh,* and *k.* This is another way of saying that the *ch, j, sh,* and *k* sounds can be spelled as *ch.* The unvoiced *ch* is a combination of *t* and *sh.* Sometimes it is pronounced as a voiced *j,* as in *spinach.* It is equivalent to *sh* in words of French derivation such as *cache, chagrin, chef, Chicago, creche, gauche, machine, machinery,* and *mustache.* It has a *k* sound in some words derived from the Greek and Hebrew as *chasm, chorus, Christ, chrism, Christmas, chrome, Enoch,* and *scheme,* and also in *ache, backache, chemist, chloride, choral, technic, technique, headache, orchid, school,* and *Czech.* In *drachm, schism, yacht,* and *fuchsia* the *ch* is silent. Here are some common words exemplifying the regular *ch* sound:

arch	change	chin	couch	leach	preach	squelch
batch	chant	chip	crotch	leech	punch	stanch
beach	chap	chirp	crutch	lunch	quench	starch
beech	charge	choice	ditch	lurch	ranch	staunch
belch	charm	choke	drench	march	reach	stench
bench	chart	choose	dutch	match	retch	stitch
birch	chase	chop	each	mooch	rich	stretch
bleach	chaste	chore	etch	much	roach	switch
blotch	chat	chose	fetch	mulch	scorch	teach
botch	cheap	chow	filch	munch	scotch	thatch
branch	cheat	chuck	flinch	notch	scratch	torch
breach	check	chug	flitch	ouch	screech	touch
breech	cheek	chum	French	parch	scrunch	trench
broach	cheer	chunk	grouch	patch	search	twitch
brooch	cheese	church	gulch	paunch	sketch	vetch
bunch	chess	churl	hatch	peach	slouch	vouch
catch	chest	churn	haunch	perch	smirch	watch
chaff	chew	cinch	hitch	pinch	smooch	welch
chain	chick	clench	hunch	pitch	smutch	winch
chair	chide	clinch	inch	poach	snatch	witch
chalk	chief	clutch	itch	pooch	snitch	wrench
champ	child	coach	latch	porch	speech	wretch
chance	chill		launch	pouch	splotch	

The Digraphs *sh* and *th*

The diagraph *sh* presents no special reading difficulties. Some common words exemplifying the sound are the following:

ash	mesh	share	shell	shop
bash	mush	shark	sherd	shorn
brash	plush	sharp	shield	short
brush	rash	shave	shift	should
bush	rush	shawl	shin	shout
cash	sash	shay	shine	shove
clash	shade	she	ship	show
dash	shaft	sheaf	shirk	shun
dish	shag	shear	shirt	slash
fish	shake	sheath	shoal	slush
flush	shale	sheathe	shoat	smash
fresh	shall	sheave	shock	splash
frosh	shalt	shed	shod	squash
gnash	sham	sheen	shoe	trash
harsh	shame	sheep	shone	wish
hush	shank	sheer	shoo	
josh	shan't	sheet	shook	
lash	shape	shelf	shoot	

The *th*, on the other hand, may be the voiceless *th* or the voiced *th*. The final *th* usually is voiceless except in *smooth*, *with*, and in *-the* endings, as in *bathe*. Some verbs (mouth, bequeath, and smooth) have dropped the final *e* but still follow the rule. Some nouns with a voiceless singular (mouth) have a voiced plural. Generally when the final *ths* is preceded by a short-vowel sound (deaths) or by a consonant (months), it is unvoiced. The words *cloths*, *truths*, *youths*, and *wreathes* may have either. Initial *th* in such words as *the*, *them*, *there*, *this*, and *thither*, is voiced. *Th* in *Thomas*, *Esther*, and *Thompson* is simply a *t*. The following words illustrate the *th* sound in monosyllabic words: Voiceless *th*

Voiceless *th*

bath	fourth	strength	thrash	thwart
berth	froth	teeth	thread	tooth
birth	growth	thank	threat	truth
booth	hath	thatch	three	twelfth
breadth	health	thaw	thresh	warmth
breath	hearth	theft	threw	wealth
broth	heath	theme	thrice	width
cloth	mirth	thick	thrift	worth
couth	mouth	thief	thrill	wraith
dearth	myth	thigh	throat	wrath
death	ninth	thin	throb	wreath
depth	north	thing	throng	youth
doth	oath	think	through	
earth	sixth	third	throw	
faith	sloth	thirst	thrush	
fifth	Smith	thong	thrust	
filth	sooth	thorn	thud	
forth	south	thought	thump	

Voiced *th*

baths	smooth	them	they	thus
bathe	soothe	then	this	thy
breathe	that	thence	those	with
clothe	the	there	thou	wreathe
scathe	thee	these	though	writhe
scythe	their			

The Digraphs *wh, gh, ph*

The combination *wh* may be pronounced as *hw* or simply as *h*. The combination *gh* may be pronounced as a simple *g*; it may be an *f*; or it may be silent. We have seen that in the combination *igh* the *gh* is silent. *Ph* commonly is an *f* sound. It also may be sounded as *v* (Stephen), as a *p* (diphthong, diphtheria, naphtha), or it may be silent (phthalein).

Here are words that illustrate the observations just made.

wh sound: whack, whale, wharf, what, wheat, wheel, wheeze, whelm, whelp, when, whence, where, whet, whew (*hwu, hu*), which, whiff, whig, while, whilst, whim, whine, whip, whirl, whish, who (hü), whoa, whole (hōl), whom (hüm), whoop (hüp), whose (hüz), why.

silent *gh*:   aught, bough, bought, brought, caught, dough, drought, eight, freight, height, light, naught, neigh, night, nought, ought, plough, sleigh, sought, straight, though, thought, through, weight, wrought.

gh as *f*:   cough, draught, laugh, rough, slough, tough, trough.

gh as *g*:   ghost, ghoul.

ph as *f*:   phase, phew, phlegm, phone, phrase, photograph, alphabet, hyphen, phonograph, phone, graph, photo, telephone, autograph, nephew, philosophy, typhoon, orphan, physics, asphalt, prophet, phobia, symphony, physical, sphere, saxophone, sophomore, geography, phonics, pamphlet, biography.

Teaching the Speech Consonants

The pupil needs to learn the speech consonants both at the beginning of a word and at the end of a word. He must learn to discriminate between the various sounds used for the same letters.

To teach the speech consonants the teacher should consult the previous exercises for consonant teaching. The following techniques may also prove useful:

1. Ask the pupil to look at a picture, say the name of the picture, and select the speech consonant that represents the beginning or end sound of the name. The first picture illustrated teaches the beginning speech consonant and the second one teaches the ending speech consonant.

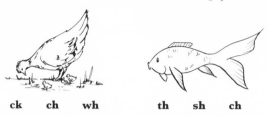

ck   ch   wh   th   sh   ch

2. Have the pupil note whether *ch* occurs at the beginning or end of a word.

chair Beginning End   **watch** Beginning End   **chicken** Beginning End

3. Ask the pupil to discriminate between the various sounds for the same blends:

> *ch:*   *ch, j, sh, k*
> *sh:*   *sh*
> *th:*   the voiced *th* and unvoiced *th*
> *wh:*   *hw* and *h*
> *gh:*   *g, f,* or silent
> *ph:*   *f, v, p,* or silent

Summary

Chapter VI surveyed the teaching of consonant blends and speech consonants both in the beginning and in the ending position.

The generalizations to be learned are best taught and learned inductively. This means frequent and varied practice. It means exposure to many different words exemplifying the generalization.

VII

THE LONG VOWELS

CHAPTER IV dealt with the teaching of the short-vowel sound. It covered the short *a* sound as in *hat*, the short *e* sound as in *met*, the short *i* sound as in *bit*, the short *o* sound as in *hot*, and the short *u* sound as in *hut*. The pupil also needs to learn the long *a* sound as in *fate* and *gaze*; the long *e* sound as in *mete*; the long *i* sound as in *bite*; the long *o* sound as in *so*, and the special *o* sounds as in *off* and in *orb*; and the long *u* sound as in *use* and *lute*. In *use* the *u* is pronounced as *yü* and in *lute* it is pronounced as *ü*. The former sound occurs regularly after *b, c, f, g, h, k, m, p*, and *v* and at the beginning of a word. After the other consonants, usage varies. The *ü* sound in common after *j, r,* and *l* when these consonants are preceded by another consonant as in *brute*. The pupil also must learn the sound of *u* in such words as *fur*.

Since the short vowel occurs much more frequently than the long vowel, the pupil customarily should sound the vowel as a short sound. If the word thus formed does not sound like a word that he already knows or if it does not make sense in the context, then another attempt must be made.

There are three principles, which should be learned inductively, that may help more advanced pupils in arriving at the correct word. These principles are the principle of variability, the principle of position, and the principle of silentness.

Before delving into these, a few observations seem in order.

1. The pupil learns vowel generalizations or rules best by *frequent* experiences with words that exemplify the rule.
2. These experiences should be consistent. Thus, any of the exceptions mentioned in this, or for that matter in any other section, should be learned as sight words.
3. Only those rules which have wide applicability are worth teaching.

The Principle of Variability

The principle of variability simply means that the pronunciation of the written vowel may change from one word to another. The *e* sound may be short as in *bed*, or long as in *he*. The pupil gradually must learn and apply the following variations:

a	*e*	*i*	*o*	*u*	*y*
a (hat	e (bed)	i (bit	ä (lot)	ə (hut	y (crypt)
ā (fade)	ē (mete)	ī (bite)	ō (so)	yü (use)	ȳ (cry)
ä (car)			ȯ (off)	ü (lute)	
e (ə) (care)			ȯ (orb)	u̇ (pull)	

The Principle of Position

The second principle simply means that the sound of the vowel changes depending upon its position in the word. By frequent exposure to monosyllabic words in which the vowel is in the beginning or medial position, the pupil should be able to formulate a principle that goes something like this: *A single vowel at the beginning or in the middle of a one-syllable word usually is short.*

The principle of position also applies in other instances. The vowel receives a long sound when a single vowel comes at the end of a one-syllable word: for example, *a, be, he, she, me, we, I, go, ho, no, so, by, cry, fly, fry, my, ply, pry, sky, sly, spry, spy, sty, try, why, wry.** A second vowel rule may be stated thus: *A single vowel at the end of a one-syllable word usually is long.*

Sometimes the vowel occurs in the middle of a word but does not follow the principle of position. The vowel is a long vowel.

long *i:* blight, bright, fight, flight, fright, high, knight, light, might, nigh, night, plight, right, sigh, sight, slight, thigh, tight, bind, blind, find, grind, hind, kind, mind, rind, wind, child, mild, wild, pint, climb.

long *o:* bold, cold, fold, gold, hold, mold, old, scold, sold, told, boll, droll, knoll, poll, roll, toll, scroll, stroll, bolt, colt, jolt, gross, ghost, host, most, post, both, comb, don't, won't.

Frequently the *o* has the *ȯ* sound of *o* and it occurs in the following words: *log, broth, cloth, froth, moth, boss, cross, dross, floss, gloss, joss, loss, moss, toss, cost, frost, lost, gong, long, prong, song, strong, throng, tong, honk, off, scoff, loft, oft, soft, cough, trough.*

For two-syllable words illustrating the vowels and vowel combinations covered in this chapter see Appendix IV.

---

* Exceptions are *ha, do, to,* and *who.*

The Principle of Silentness

The third principle to be learned is that of silentness. Some vowels in words are not pronounced. When the letter *e* comes at the end of a monosyllabic word, it frequently is silent. In addition, the normally short sound in the middle of the word becomes a long vowel. A third rule may be stated thus: In one-syllable words in which there are two vowels, the second one being a silent *e* preceded by a single consonant, the initial vowel is long. Emans[24] reports that this rule has about 70 per cent utility if words ending in *le* (ankle) and *ive* (live) are accepted as exceptions to it.

Since the pupil has heard and spoken many monosyllabic words that exemplify this rule, it is desirable to consider such words next. Table VI lists words that follow this principle. Teaching of the long vowel sounds may begin with the words in Table VI.

TABLE VI

MONOSYLLABIC WORDS WITH A SILENT E AT THE END AND A LONG-VOWEL SOUND
IN THE BEGINNING OR MIDDLE OF THE WORD

ape	crime	flame	lane	node	ride	smite	time
ate	crude	fluke	late	nose	rife	smoke	tire
babe	cruse	fuse	life	note	rile	smote	tome
bake	cube	gale	line	nude	rime	snake	tone
bale	cute	game	lobe	ode	ripe	snipe	tote
bane	dame	gape	lode	pale	rise	snore	trade
base	Dane	gate	lone	pane	rite	sole	tribe
bate	date	glade	lube	Pete	robe	spade	tripe
bibe	dime	grate	lure	pike	rode	spate	tube
bide	dine	grime	lute	pile	role	spike	tune
bike	dire	gripe	made	pine	rope	spine	twine
bile	dome	grope	make	pipe	rude	spire	vale
bite	dope	hate	mane	plane	rule	spite	vane
blade	dose	hide	mate	plate	safe	spume	vile
blame	dote	hike	mete	plebe	sake	stake	vine
bone	drape	hire	Mike	plume	sale	stale	vise
bore	drive	hole	mike	poke	sate	stile	vote
bride	drove	home	mile	pole	scale	stipe	wade
brine	dude	hone	mine	pope	scape	stoke	wake
brute	duke	hope	mire	pose	scope	stole	wane
cake	dupe	hose	mite	prime	shake	sure	waste
came	eke	jade	mode	probe	side	swine	wide
cane	fade	Jane	mole	prone	sire	swipe	wife
cape	fake	jibe	mope	prose	site	take	wile
chore	fame	joke	mote	prune	skate	tale	wine
clove	fate	Jude	mule	pure	slate	tame	wipe
code	fife	June	muse	quite	slide	tape	wire
coke	file	Kate	mute	quote	slime	tide	wise
cone	fine	kite	name	rake	slope	tike	yoke
cope	fire	lake	nape	rape	smile	tile	Yule
crate	flake	lame	nine	rate			

The following words are exceptions and should be learned by sight: *are* (ar), *come* (kəm), *done* (dən), *dove* (dəv), *give* (giv), *gone* (gȯn), *have* (hav), *move* (müv), *none* (nən), *one* (wən), *some* (səm), and *were* (wər). *O* frequently is a short *u* as in *some, come, dove, love, done, none, one.*

A new sound occurs in the following words: *bare, blare, care, dare, fare, flare, glare, hare, mare, pare, rare, scare, snare, spare, stare,* and *ware.* This *a e*(ə) is a more open sound than the long *a* sound and occurs commonly in accented syllables and/or in conjunction with the *r* round. There is no great need to distinguish it for the pupil from the long *a* sound.

The pupil must learn further extensions of the principle of silentness.

In certain vowel combinations, for example, *ai, ay, ea, ee, oa, oe,* and *ow,* the second letter may be silent and the first is long. Here are various monosyllabic words that follow this rule:

Ai as *ā*	plaint	may	flee	seen	coat	foe
	praise	nay	fleet	seep	croak	goes
aid	quail	play		sleek	float	hoe
aide	quaint	pray	geese	sleep	foal	Joe
ail	raid	ray	Greek	sleet	goam	toe
aim	rain	say	green	speed	gloam	woe
bail	raise	slay	greet	steed	gloat	
bait	sail	stay	heed	steel	goad	*Ow* as *ō*
braid	saint	tray	heel	steep	goal	
brail	slain	way	jeep	sweep	goat	blow
brain	snail		keel	sweet	groan	bow
claim	staid	*Ee* as *ē*	keep	teem	load	bowl
drain	stain		knee	teens	loaf	crow
fail	tail	bee	kneel	tree	loam	flow
fain	taint	beech	leek	tweed	loan	flown
faint	trail	beef	lees	tweet	moan	glow
flail	train	beet	meet	wee	moat	grow
gain	trait	bleed	need	weed	oak	grown
gait	waif	breed	peek	week	oat	know
hail	wail	creed	peel	weep	road	low
jail	waist	creek	peep		roam	mow
laid	wait	creel	preen	*Oa* as *ō*	roan	owe
lain		creep	queen		roast	own
maid	*Ay* as *ā*	creese	reed	boar	soak	row
mail		deed	reef	board	soap	show
maim	bay	deem	reek	boast	toad	slow
main	clay	deep	reel	boat	toast	snow
maize	day	eel	see	cloak		stow
paid	flay	feed	seed	coal		throw
pail	gay	feel		coast	doe	tow
paint	hay	feet	seem			

Some exceptions to this rule are *aisle* (īl), *plaid* (plad), *said* (sed), *aye* (ī), *says* (sez), *been* (bin), *broad* (brȯd), *does* (dəz), *shoe* (shü). The *ee* followed by *r* is always *i*(ə).

In an analysis of vowel-vowel combinations which have one sound, Burmeister[13] found that the *ai* combination has the long *a* sound 74 per cent of the time; in 16 per cent of the cases, it is followed by *r* and is pronounced *e(ə)* as in *air* or *chair*. Emans[24] found that *ai* was pronounced as long *a* 83 per cent of the time. There are obviously going to be variations in these findings because of differences in types of materials from which words are taken, in method of word selection, in phonemic systems, and in definition of what is a short and a long vowel.[12] The exceptions should be learned as sight words: *aisle, plaid, said, mountain, villain, again*.

The *ay* combination has a long *a* sound almost 95 per cent of the time;[13] common exceptions are *aye, says, yesterday*.

The *ee* combination is pronounced as long *e* about 85 per cent of the time;[13] the words *beer, cheer, deer, jeer, peer, queer, sheer, sneer, steer*, and *veer*, have the *i* (ə) sound. This is a lowered long *e* sound and occurs only in conjunction with *r*. It occurs about 12 per cent of the time.[13] A common exception is *been*.

The *oa* combination is sounded like a long *o* 94 per cent of the time. The *oa*, pronounced as in *broad*, occurs the remaining 6 per cent of the time.

The *oe* combination occurs much less frequently than *oa* and its pronunciation is much less consistent. It is pronounced as long *o* 60 per cent of the time; as long *e* 23 per cent of the time, and as $\overline{oo}$, in such words as *shoe, snowshoe, canoe*, and *horseshoe*, 18 per cent of the time.[13] A common exception is *does*.

The *ow* combination is listed here because in some instances it follows the general principle of silentness. In *ow*, the *w* is not pronounced and the *o* is given its long sound 50 per cent of the time. It is pronounced as *ow* as in *town*, 48 per cent of the time.

The principle of silentness also applies to certain words having an *ea* combination. This group of words is by far the least consistent. The pupil will have to learn many of the words as sight words. In attacking words with the *ea* combination the pupil's best guess is the long *e* sound. It occurs about 50 per cent of the time.[13] The next most common usage is that of the short *e* as in *bread*. The short-vowel sound can be represented by various vowel combinations (see Appendix III). In this instance the short *e* sound is written *ea*.

The pupil must learn that *break, great*, and *steak* are pronounced as

brāk, grāt, and *stāk.* The ending -*ear* may be pronounced four ways:
as *i*(ə) in *beard, clear, dear, ear, fear, gear, hear, near, rear, sear, shear,
smear,* and *spear;* as *e*(ə) in *bear, pear, swear, wear;* as *ə* in *dearth, earl,
earn, earth, hearse,* and *pearl;* and as *ä* in *heart* and *hearth.* See Table
VII for the various pronunciations for *ea,* omitting the long *e* sound.

TABLE VII

			*Ea**		
	Ea			*Ear*	
e	*ā*	*i*(ə)	*e*(ə)	*ə*	*ä*
bread	great	clear	bear	earl	heart
breadth	break	dear	pear	dearth	hearth
breast	steak	beard	swear	earn	
breath		ear	wear	earth	
dead		fear		hearse	
deaf		gear		pearl	
dealt		hear		search	
death		near			
dread		rear			
dreamt		sear			
head		shear			
health		smear			
lead		spear			
meant		tear			
read					
realm					
spread					
stealth					
sweat					
thread					
threat					
tread					
wealth					

* Some two-syllable words with *ea* pronounced as short e are *abreast, headache, ahead, already, baldhead, behead, blockhead, breakfast, bullhead, deadbeat, deaden, deadeye, deadly, deafen, deafmute, dreadful, feather, headlight, headlong, headstrong, healthful, healthy, heaven, heavy, hothead, instead, jealous, leather, meadow, measure, pleasant, peasant, pleasure, ready, redhead, retread, steady, sweater, threaten, weapon, weather, wealthy.* In *heartbreak* and *heartburn,* it is *ä.* In *impearl, learned, rehearse, searching, unearth,* and *research* it is *ə.*

The following *ea* combinations are pronounced as long *e:*

beach	beast	breach	cleave	dean	eat	gleam
bead	beat	breathe	creak	dream	feast	glean
beak	bleach	cheap	cream	each	feat	grease
beam	bleak	clean	crease	ease	flea	greave
bean	bleat	cheat	deal	east	freak	heal

heap	leak	peach	reach	seam	squeal	treat
heat	lean	peak	read	seat	steal	veal
heath	leap	peaked	ream	sheaf	steam	weak
heave	lease	peal	reap	sheath	streak	weal
jean	leave	peat	reave	sheathe	stream	weave
knead	meal	plea	screak	sheave	tea	wheat
lea	mean	plead	scream	sleave	teach	wreak
lead	neat	please	sea	sneak	team	wreath
leaf	pea	pleat	seal	speak	tease	wreathe
league	peace	preach				

The Diphthongs

Diphthongs are vowel combinations that have a single sound. The sound is distinct from that represented by either of the single letters. The most common such combinations are *au, aw, oi, oy,* and *oo.*

Au **and** *aw*

The combination *au* is pronounced *ò* (ought) 94 per cent of the time;[13] the principal exceptions are *draught, gauge, aunt, chauffeur,* and *laugh. Aw* is pronounced as *ò* (law) 100 per cent of the time[13] when it occurs at the end of the word or syllable or is followed by *k, l,* or *n.*

> *Au* as *ò:* aught, caught, caulk, cause, craunch, daub, daunt, fault, faun, flaunt, fraud, Gaul, gaunt, gauze, haul, haunch, haunt, jaunt, laud, launch, mauve, naught, naughty, Paul, paunch, pause, sauce, Saul, staunch, taught, taunt, vault, vaunt, applaud, applause, assault, auburn, audit, auger, augment, augur, August, austere, auto, because, caucus, causal, dauntless, default, defraud, laundress, naughty, saucepan, saucer, saucy, slaughter.

> *Aw* as *ò:* awe, awl, awn, bawl, brawl, brawn, claw, craw, crawl, dawn, draw, drawl, drawn, fawn, flaw, gawk, hawk, jaw, law, lawn, paw, pawn, raw, saw, scrawl, shawl, slaw, spawn, sprawl, squaw, squawk, straw, thaw, trawl, awesome, brawny, awful, awning, bylaw, drawer, drawing, gnawing, hacksaw, inlaw, jigsaw, lawful, lawless, lawsuit, lawyer, pawnshop, rawhide, tawny.

Oi **and** *oy*

The sound of *oi* as in *boil* is consistent 98 per cent of the time.[13] It occurs in the following monosyllabic words: *boil, broil, choice, coil, coin, droit, foil, foist, hoist, join, joint, joist, moist, noise, oil, point, poise, soil, spoil, toil, voice, void, appoint, avoid, boiler, cloister, foible, jointly, jointweed, noisy, recoil, rejoice, rejoin, toilet, toiler, topsoil, uncoil,* and *unsoiled.* A common exception is *choir.*

The sound of *oy* as in *boy* also is regular 98 per cent of the time. Common words are *coy, joy, Roy, soy, toy, Troy, alloy, bellboy, boycott, boyhood, boyish, convoy, cowboy, decoy, deploy, destroy, enjoy, envoy, joyful, loyal, oyster, royal,* and *tomboy.* An exception is *coyote.*

The Combination *oo*

Oo is pronounced as *ü* (bloom) 59 per cent of the time;[13] as *u* (cook), 36 per cent of the time;[13] as *o* (door), and as short *u* (blood). The latter two occur infrequently and should be taught as exceptions. Emans[24] found that the *ü* sound occurred 74 per cent of the time in his study; the *u* sound, 26 per cent. The combination *ook* occurs frequently enough in words that one may speak of the *ook* words. Some examples are *book, brook, cook, crook, hook, nook, rook, shook,* and *took.* Only *spook* is an exception.

The following words are illustrative of the *oo* combinations:

oo as *ü :*   bloom, boo, boom, boon, boost, boot, booth, booze, brood, broom, choose, coo, cool, coon, coop, coot, croon, doom, drool, droop, food, fool, gloom, goof, goon, goose, groom, groove, hoof, hoop, moo, mooch, mood, moon, moose, moot, noose, pooch, pool, proof, roof, room, roost, root, school, scoop, scoot, shoo, shoot, sloop, smooch, smooth, snoop, snoot, snooze, soon, sooth, soothe, spook, spool, spoon, stooge, stoop, swoon, swoop, too, tool, toot, tooth, troop, whoop, zoo, zoom, baboon, balloon, ballroom, bamboo, bassoon, bedroom, behoove, blooming, booby, booster, bootleg, bridegroom, caboose, cartoon, classroom, cocoon, cooler, coolie, disproof, doodle, fooling, foodstuff, foolish, gloomy, homeroom, igloo, moonlight, moonshine, mushroom, noodle, noonday, noontime, papoose, platoon, raccoon, reproof, roofing, roomette, roommate, rooster, rootbeer, saloon, storeroom, toothache, toothbrush, toothpick.

oo as *u :*   barefoot, bookend, bookmark, bookworm, childhood, cookbook, football, footbridge, foothill, footnote, girlhood, goodness, lookout, manhood, redwood, rookie, sooty, woodpile, woodshed, woodsman, woodwork, lookout, book, brook, cook, crook, foot, good, hood, hook, look, nook, shook, soot, stood, took, wood, wool.

oo as *ō :*   brooch, door, floor, doorstep, doorway, doorsill.

oo as short *u :*   blood, flood, bloodshed, bloodshot, bloodstain, bloody, floodlight.

Other Vowel Combinations

There are a number of other vowel combinations which occur frequently enough to be included in this survey. They are *ei*, *ey*, *ew*, *ie*, *ou*, *ow*, *ue*, and *ui*.

Ei (ey)

A common pronunciation for *ei* is that of a long *a*. It occurs 40 per cent of the time.[13] The following words are illustrative: *beige, deign, feign, feint, reign, rein, reindeer, seine, skein, veil, vein, eight, freight, neigh, sleigh, weigh*, and *weight*.

In about 26 per cent of the cases, *ei* is simply pronounced as a long *e*, the second vowel being silent: *ceiling, deceive, conceive, receive, perceive, leisure, seize, either, neither*.

The *ei* may be pronounced as long *i* (height), short *e* (heifer), and short *i* (forfeit, sovereign).

The *ey* is pronounced as short *i* 58 per cent of the time:[13] barley, honey, kidney, parley. It is pronounced as long *a* 20 percent of the time:[13] *hey, obey, prey, they, whey*. It occurs as long *i*: *eye, eyeball, eyebrow, eyelash*, and as long *e*: *key, keyboard, keyhole, passkey*.

Ie

Ie generally is a long *e* (36 per cent of the time), a short *i* (19 per cent), or a long *i* (17 per cent).[13] The long *i* sound is common when *ie* is at the end of a word and in the ending *ied*. The following words are illustrative of the various ounds for *ie*:

Long *e*: brief, chief, fief, field, fiend, frieze, grief, grieve, lief, liege, mien, niece, piece, priest, shield, shriek, siege, thief, wield, yield, achieve, backfield, belief, believe, grievance, grievous, hygiene, priestly, rabies, relief, retrieve, timepiece, wieldy.

Long *i*: die, fie, flied, fried, lie, pie, tried, vie, allied, applied, belie, implied, tie-up, untie, untried.

Short *e*: friend, befriend, friendless, friendly, friendship.

Short *i*: sieve.

The Combination *ou*

Ou has numerous pronunciations: as *ou* in *blouse;* as long *o* in *course;* as *ü* in *coop;* as *u* in *could;* as *o* in *bought;* as short *u* in *touch*, and as *ò* in *cough*. Certainly, the most common sounds are *ou*, 35 per cent of the time;[13] as the schwa sound of *ou* in rigorous, 41 per cent; as *ü* (soup), 7 per cent; and as *ō*, 6 per cent. The child should learn the *ought* words and the *could* words. He must learn the pronunciation of such common words as *tough, cough, tour,* and *your.*

The following words may be used to teach the various sounds:

ou as *ou:*   blouse, bough, bounce, bound, bout, cloud, clout, couch, count, crouch, douse, drought, flounce, flour, foul, found, fount, gouge, gout, grouch, ground, hound, hour, house, loud, mound, mount, mouse, mouth, noun, ouch, ounce, our, oust, out, pouch, plough, pounce, pound, pout, proud, round, rout, scour, scout, shout, shroud, abound, about, account, aground, aloud, around, arouse, astound, background, blockhouse, blowout, bouncing, bounty, cloudburst, cloudy, compound, counsel, county, devour, devout, discount, doghouse, enounce, flounder, greenhouse, greyhound, guardhouse, housecoat, household, housemaid, housewife, housework, icehouse, mountain, mounted, mounting, mouthful, ourself, ouster, outboard, outbreak, outburst, outcome, outcry, outdoors, outer, outfit, outing, outlaw, outlay, outlet, outlive, outmost, outpost, output, outrage, outright, outsell, outshine, outside, outskirt, outsmart, outward, outwards, outweigh, outwork, playhouse, pronoun, pronounce, propound, recount, renounce, rounding, roundness, roundup, rousing, southwest, stoutness, trousers.

ou as *ō:*   course, court, dough, four, fourth, furlough, mould, mourn, pour, soul, source, though, although, doughnut, thorough, courtroom, courtship, courtyard, discourse, doughnut, fourteen, fourthly, mourning, poultry, recourse, resource.

ou as *ü:*   coup, couth, croup, ghoul, group, rouge, route, soup, through, wound, you, youth, cougar, coupon, detour.

ou as short *u:* cousin, country, couple, double, enough, tough, rough, roughage, roughen, roughly, roughness, touch, trouble, young, famous, touchback, touchy, toughen, grievous, jealous, monstrous, pious.

ou as *ȯ:*   bought, brought, cough, nought, fought, ought, sought, thought, wrought.

ou as *u̇:*   could, should, tour, would, your.

ou as *ə:*   adjourn, journal, journey, flourish.

The Combination *ow*

The pupil already has learned the long *o* sound of *ow*. He also must learn the *ou* sound of *ow*. This sound at the end of the word usually is written as *ow* and occurs in the following words:

bow, brow, brown, browse, chow, clown, cow, cowl, crowd, crown, down, dowse, drown, drowse, frown, gown, growl, how, howl, jowl, owl, plow, prow, prowl, scowl, sow, town, wow, allow, avow, backdown, breakdown, chowchow, cowbell, cowbird, cowboy, cowhide, dowry, endow, flower, Howard, howdy, nightgown, powder, power, powwow, prowess, renowned, towel, tower, township, uptown.

The Combinations *ew, ue, ui*

The pupil has learned two sounds for the long *u*: the *yü* sound and the *ü* sound after *j, r, bl, fl, pl, cl, gl*, and *sl*. The *yü* sound is regularly used after *b, c, f, g, h, k, m, p*, and *v*. He must apply the same principles to the *ew, ue, w*, and *ew* combinations:

ew as *yü*: ewe, few, hew, lewd, mew, new, pew, phew, skew, spew, stew, thew, view, whew, sinew, askew, nephew, newly, newness, renew, review.

ew as *ü*: blew, brew, crew, drew, flew, grew, Jew, screw, shrewd, slew, threw, Hebrew, jewel, Jewess.

ue as *yü*: cue, due, hue, imbue.

ue as *ü* blue, clue, flue, glue, rue, sue, slue, true, accrue, bluegill, bluegrass, blueprint, construe, gruesome, rueful, untrue, statue, tissue.

ui as *yü*: nuisance.

ui as *ü*: bruise, cruise, juice, sluice, suit, grapefruit, fruitcake, juicy, recruit.

eu as *yü*: deuce, feud, Europe, feudal, Teuton, neural, neuter, neutral, neutron.

The *yü* sound of *ew* occurs 61 per cent of the time; the *ü* sound, 34 per cent.[13] *Ew* also occurs as long *o* (sew).

The *yü* sound of *ue* occurs 63 per cent of the time; the *ü* sound, 37 per cent of the time.[13]

The *yü* sound of *ui* occurs 24 per cent of the time; the *ü* sound, 29 per cent; and the short *i* sound, 47 per cent.[13] Emans[24] found in his study that *ui* had a short *i* sound 79 per cent of the time (build, built, guilt, guilty, building). An exception is *suite*.

The *yü* sound of *eu* occurs 72 per cent of the time.[13]

The vowel combinations in order of frequency of occurrence according to Burmeister[13] are *ou, ea, ai, oo, ee, ow, au, ie, oa, ay, oi, ei, aw, ey, ew, oy, ue, eu, ui,* and *oe.*

Teaching the Long Vowels

Burmeister[13] points out that phonemes for vowel pairs tend to fall into the following categories:

1. The first vowel may do the talking as in *ai, ay, ea, ee, oa,* or *ow* and say its name. *Ea* may be long *e* or short *e; ow* may be long *o* or *ou.*
2. The two vowels may blend (*au, aw, oi, oy, oo*); *oo* may sound as in *lagoon* or *wood.*
3. The two vowels may create a new sound (*ei, ow, ey, ew*).

Sabaroff[48] identifies five basic vowel patterns:

1. The single (or short) vowel pattern as in *bat* or *at.*
2. The open-vowel pattern as in *he, she,* or *me.*
3. The vowel with final *e* pattern as in *rope* or *use.*
4. The double-vowel pattern as in *rain.*
5. The modified-vowel pattern as in bird, *word,* or a*ll.*

He points out that instruction should begin with words in pattern 1.

The pupil needs to learn the basic generalizations that govern sounding. The child should see how the rule fits the words that he has learned. He should be asked to provide other words that follow the same rule.

Perhaps the sound of the individual vowels is best learned through practice with actual words. However, the rules and principles have their value. In fact, generalizations are not necessarily learned best inductively. If this were so, many theories would forever elude us. Sometimes, it seems to be more effective to state the generalization explicitly.

When the vowels are being taught, the child initially looks at a picture, pronounces its name, and identifies the short sound. The teacher may ask, "What vowel sound occurs in the word *cat?* In the word *bell?*

Next the pupil should be taught to discriminate between the short and the long vowel. What sound occurs in the word *mule?* In the word *go?* Are these short sounds or long sounds? Why? The teacher asks the child to look at words like *came, flame,* and *dame.* How many vowels are pronounced? Which vowel is silent? What happens to the first vowel when the *e* is silent and is preceded by a single consonant?

Exercises such as the following are especially helpful in teaching the various vowel sounds.

1. Have the pupil look at the pictures below. Note that each has the long *a* sound as in *cake* and the *a* is followed by a consonant and a silent *e*.

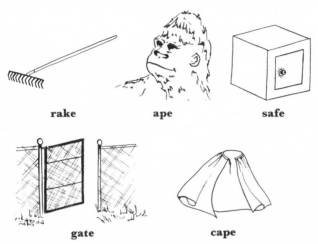

rake	ape	safe

gate	cape

2. Have the child memorize a little ditty such as the following:

A is called ă,
When it tells of the cat,
Which stumbled and fell
When chasing the rat.

A is called ā,
When it tells of the cake
That Mama is going to bake
And that I will help her make.

3. Have the pupil put a line through each picture that has a long *a* sound.

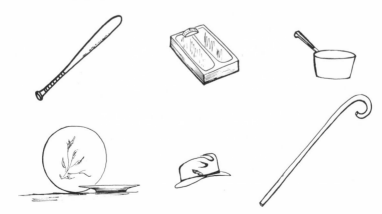

4. Have the pupil circle the correct *a* sound.

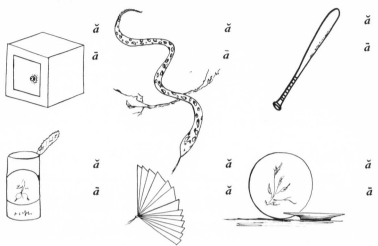

5. Have the pupil write the missing vowels. This exercise is useful in teaching long vowels followed by silent *e*.

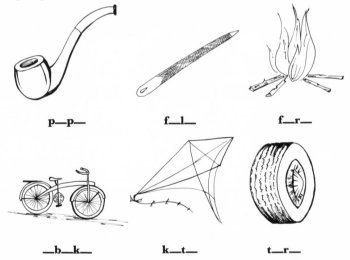

6. Have pupils turn words such as *at, bad, ban, bat, bib, bid, cam, can, cap, cod, cop, cub, cut, dam, Dan, dim, din, dot, fat, grim, grip, hat, hid, hop, Jan, kit, mad, man, mat, met, mop, nap, not, pal, pan, pin, pip,* or *pop* into other words by adding an *e*.

7. Provide a list of words with the long vowel missing and let them add it: *b-, cr-, pl-te, b-ke, c-ke, d-me.*

8. Have pupil write the word that rhymes with the picture. (This teaches long vowel plus silent *e*).

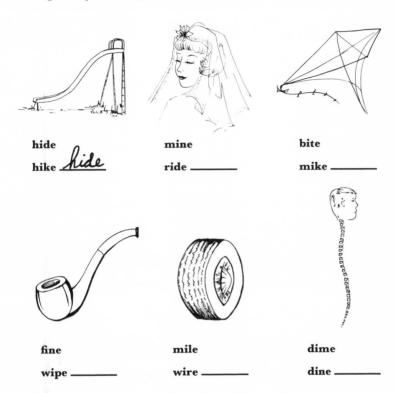

hide
hike *hide*

mine
ride _____

bite
mike _____

fine
wipe _____

mile
wire _____

dime
dine _____

9. Have pupils write the missing ending. (This teaches long vowel plus silent *e*).

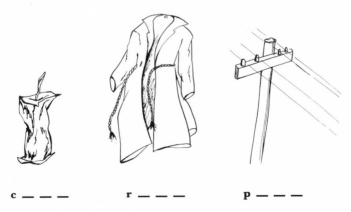

c _ _ _   **r** _ _ _   **p** _ _ _

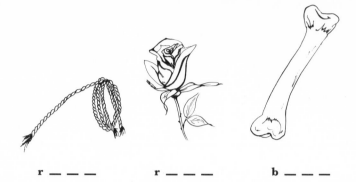

r _ _ _   r _ _ _ _   b _ _ _

10. Have pupils fill in the blank with one of the words on top of the exercise.

        Go,   No,   So,   Do,   To

    a. Bob will _____ home.

    b. Will you sing? _____, I will not.

    c. Dad has to go _____ the bank.

    d. Jim is _____ sick that he cannot get up.

11. Have pupils indicate by number the picture that has the same vowel sound as the word.

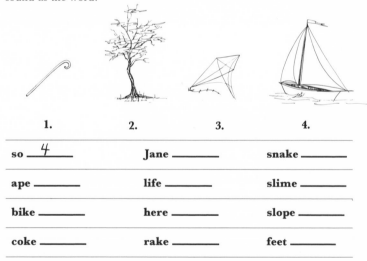

    1.   **2.**   **3.**   **4.**

so _4_	Jane _____	snake _____
ape _____	life _____	slime _____
bike _____	here _____	slope _____
coke _____	rake _____	feet _____

12. Since the long sound of *y* has been introduced in words like *cry, fly, my*, the pupil should be taught the difference between the long and short *i* sound of *y*. The following words are helpful in demonstrating this: *bye, dye, dyke, pyre, rhyme, rye, style, tyke, type, crypt, myth, rhythm.*

13. The pupil, besides learning to discriminate between long and short vowels, needs to learn how to designate long and short vowels and how to

indicate silent letters. An exercise like the following teaches this.

āt¢	blow	hay	fan
hot	got	duke	jail
dīn¢	soap	bed	see
gō	sleep	fun	rake
get	joke	fame	brute
fēȧst	tube	Brad	name
cut	bike	sat	like

14. Have pupils circle the correct word in exercises such as the following:

a. He kicks the ball **at / ate** the wall.

b. He **at / ate** the fish.

c. The **can / cane** is full of fish.

d. He walks with a **can. / cane.**

e. His leg is **lam. / lame.**

f. Jim made a big **fir / fire** in a pit.

15. Have pupils write in the correct word.

a. Here are _____ men.

b. Pam is baking a _____ **in a stove.**

c. He put the _____ **on her and got her all wet.**

16. Have the pupil match the vowel sound in a picture with a sound that he already knows:

cow (ou)	**bow (ō)**
1. snow __ō__	6. plow _____
2. down _____	7. blow _____
3. owl _____	8. clown _____
4. gown _____	9. how _____
5. brown _____	10. slow _____

17. Have the pupil select the correct pronunciation for a given vowel combination.

18. Have pupils learn phonograms; for example, *ite, cat, ike, ail.*

The Effect of *r* on a Preceding Vowel

The pupil also must be able to cope with *ar, er, or, ir,* and *ur.* The consonant sometimes influences the sound of the vowel. The letter *r*, when following a single vowel, changes the sound of the vowel. The vowel is neither long nor short. Bailey[3] found that this generalization was true 86 per cent of the time. The pupil already has some experience with this phenomenon. The *a* in monosyllables when followed by *r* or when followed by *r* plus another consonant is the *ä* sound (bar, car, art, arm, far, mar).

Unfortunately, not all *a*'s followed by *r* are pronounced as *ä*. When the *r* is followed by a silent *e* (care, fare) or when it is the final letter in an accented syllable and is followed by a vowel (parent, Mary), the *a* frequently is pronounced *e(ə)*. However, the *a* may be a short vowel in this last instance (paradise, paradox). When the *a* is the final letter is an unaccented syllable and is followed by an *r* in the next syllable it is *ə* (maroon, cataract).

In the suffix *ar*, as in *ward*, and in some final syllables, *ar* is pronounced (*ə*)*r* (lair, granular, westward, pillar, dollar, orchard, Tartar, circular, lizard, sugar, grammar, collar, wizard, lizard, mustard). In the suffix *ary*, *ar* is pronounced as *er* (stationary, legendary, sanitary).

Er in monosyllabic words (her), generally in accented syllables (revert), and in unaccented syllables in which the *er* is followed by a consonant (adverb) is sounded as *ər*. When it names a person (baker) or has a comparative meaning (hotter), it is usually pronounced as (*ə*)*r*. It may also be *er*(meridian), *i*(*ə*) (here), or *e*(*ə*) (there, where, ferry, herring, very, perish).

Ir is sounded as *ər* in monosyllables (firm) and in accented syllables (firkin). It may be sounded as *ə*(*r*) (tapir), *ī*r (dire), or *ir* (virile, irrelevant, irritate).

Or is sounded as *ər* when *or* follows *w* as in word. In other monosyllabic words it is sounded as *ō* or as *ŏ*. The *or* may be pronounced as *ə*(*r*) (inventor) or may become *ŏr* or *ŏr* (coral, torrid). It usually is pronounced *ə*(*r*) when it names a person (doctor) or a quality or condition (horror).

Ur is sounded as *ər* in monosyllabic words and in the accented syllable of polysyllabic words. *Ur* also may be *ə*(*r*) (liturgy), *ŭr* (cure), and *ŭ* (sure, jury, hurrah, rural).

When *ar*, *er*, *ir*, *or*, or *ur* are followed by a second *r*, the vowel is usually short (barrel, barren, sparrow, arrest, barrack, derrick, error, terrier, errand, mirror, borrow, horror, sorry, corrupt, torrent, torrid).

The vowel also is short when the *r* is followed by a vowel (charity, tariff, lariat, parachute, paratroop, parasol, parapet, parallel, parasite, parable, ceremony, America, very, inherit, peril, verify, merit, cleric, spirit, miracle, direct, quorum).

Sometimes the *r* is separated from the vowel preceding it and has no effect on its pronunciation (arise, around, arena, spiral, Irish, erect, erupt, hero, irate, siren, uranium, pirate, virus, furious, spirant, wiry, glory, tyrant, mores, oral, story, Tory).

The following lists of words illustrate the various combinations of the vowel with the *r* in monosyllabic words:

er as *ər:*   berg, berth, clerk, err, erst, fern, germ, her, herd, jerk, kern, merge, nerve, per, perch, perk, pert, serf, serge, serve, sherd, stern, swerve, term, tern, verge, verse, versed, wert.

ir as *ər:*   birch, bird, birth, chirp, dirge, dirt, fir, firm, firn,* first, flirt, firth, gird, girl, girt, girth, irk, Kirk, mirk, mirth, quirk, shirk, shirt, skirt, squirm, squirt, stir, third, twirl, whirl.

or as *ò:*   born, cord, cork, corn, for, gorge, horn, horse, Lord, morn, Morse, norm, Norse, north, or, orb, scorch, scorn, short, snort, sort, sport, stork, storm, torch, tort, worn.

or as *ər:*   word, work, world, worm, worse, worst, wort, worth.

ur as *ər:*   blur, blurb, blurt, burg, burn, burnt, burp, burr, burse, burst, church, churn, curb, curd, curl, curse, curt, curve, durst, fur, furl, gurge, hurl, hurt, lurch, lurk, nurse, purge, purse, scurf, slur, spur, spurge, spurn, spurt, surf, surge, turf, Turk, turn, urge, urn.

Summary

Chapter VII completes for the most part the teaching of vowel sounds, especially as they function in monosyllabic words. The materials presented in this section should be taught inductively and only gradually. Only with a lot of experience will the pupil come to master them.

---

* Firn has a short *i*.

VIII

TEACHING STRUCTURAL-ANALYSIS

STRUCTURAL analysis is possible with three kinds of words: (1) ones that have an inflectional ending such as *s*, *es*, *ed*, or *ing*, (2) derived words, being constructed from root, suffix and/or prefix, or (3) compound words.

In the initial stage the child commonly is introduced to two kinds of words which may be analyzed structurally. The child learns that the *s* can change the word in two ways: (1) It changes the verb into third person singular and (2) it makes a noun plural in form. The teaching of the *s* plural is easier when it is accompanied by another word in the sentence that suggests the plural. The sentence *Tom has ten pet pups* is an example of this.

As the pupil's skill in structural analysis develops, he may identify two simple words in one larger word. He may see *tea* and *pot* in *teapot; some* and *thing* in *something ;* or *bat* and *boy* in *batboy*.

Frequently, he may be able to identify by sight only one of the two words and will identify the other through picture reading, contextual clues, or phonetic clues. The ability to see little words—and they should be words—in bigger words is helpful in pronouncing the word.

And he gradually learns to break the word into its syllables and to handle words composed of roots, prefixes, and suffixes.

Syllabication must receive attention at all levels of reading instruction. For most pupils, learning in this area is greatest during the intermediate grades. However, even in the first grade the pupil must be trained to hear and see the distinct vowel sounds that occur in a word. Gradually, some children will learn that the number of vowel sounds indicates the number of syllables in a word.

102

In the primary grades structural analysis is the following:

1. Teaching of the common word ending *s*.
2. Teaching the compounds such as *gunman, hotdog*.
3. Teaching two-syllable words—beginning with words ending in *ing*.
4. Teaching the past tense with *ed*.
5. Teaching the plural with *es*.
6. Teaching simple prefixes and suffixes.
7. Teaching the apostrophe *s*.
8. Teaching simple syllabication.

Hanson[29] found that variant endings (*s*, *ing*, *ed*, *er*) can be taught in first grade and should be used in preprimers, primers, and first readers. He reports on studies by Dolch and Osborne which point out that the three most common syllables are *ing*, *ed*, and *er*. A child who early learns *ing* will be able to transfer this knowledge to hundreds of words.

Betts[7] has outlined the steps in applying phonics skills to the syllables of words:

1. The pupil must first learn to hear the number of syllables in spoken words.
2. He must learn to identify syllables in printed words. Early in the grades the pupil needs to learn that some words ending in *ed* have only one syllable (cooked); other have two syllables (landed).
3. He must learn to accent the proper syllable. Accentuation should be taught only after the pupil has mastered steps one and two and after having learned something about prefixes and suffixes. These latter rarely are accented (*in*tend, fish*ing*).
4. He must learn to apply phonic skills to the separate vowels in words.
   a. He applies the short-vowel rule to the stressed syllable (rabbit).
   b. He identifies such vowel-phonograms as *ar, er, ir, or, ur*.
5. He must check if the word makes sense in the sentence.

Let us look more closely at each of the above eight teaching tasks.

Teaching Ending S

The *s* may be used to form the third person singular of a verb or to convert a noun into its plural form. Beginning with the vocabulary that the pupil already knows, the pupil is shown what the addition of *s* does to the word. Here are examples of both uses:

s with a verb		*s with a noun*		
bats	jabs	bibs	cobs	jobs
bets	jigs	buns	cubs	pigs
bids	mops	bags	cups	nets
cuts	nabs	beds	dens	nuts

digs	pets		buds	dogs	pans
dims	tags		bugs	guns	pens
gets	taps		cabs	hats	pins
hits	tips		cans	hens	pots
hops	tugs		caps	huts	pups
hugs	wins		cats	hogs	

Exercises like the following teach the use of the third person singular *s* and the plural *s*.

Teaching Third Person Singular *s*

1. Have the pupil circle the correct verb in an exercise such as the following:

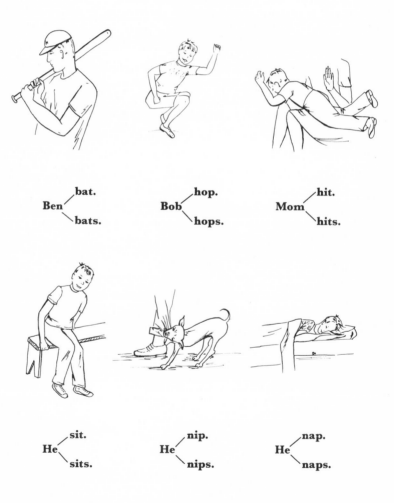

Ben < bat. / bats.   Bob < hop. / hops.   Mom < hit. / hits.

He < sit. / sits.   He < nip. / nips.   He < nap. / naps.

2. Have the pupil put a circle around the correct word in exercises like the following:

a. The cop ⟨nab / nabs⟩ the man.

b. Nan ⟨mop / mops⟩ the mat.

c. He ⟨hit / hits⟩ the ball.

Teaching the Plural *s*

1. Have the pupil circle the correct word in an exercise such as the following:

nut   nuts   hen   hens   mat   mats

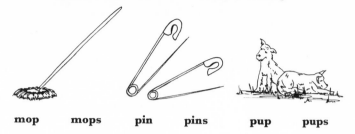

mop   mops   pin   pins   pup   pups

2. Have the pupil put a circle around the correct word in exercises such as the following:

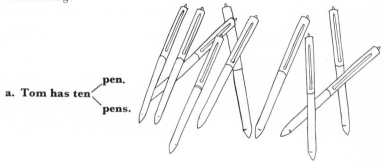

a. Tom has ten pen.
                    pens.

b. The pup
           pups **are on a cot.**

c. The cup
           cups **are tan.**

Teaching the Pronunciation of *s*

S presents also a prenunication problem for the pupil. He must decide whether the *s* is pronounced as *s* or as *z*. Table VIII illustrates when the *s* or the *z* is the appropriate pronunciation.

TABLE VIII

THE SOUND OF S

S IS PRONOUNCED			
s	after	{ *f, k, p, t,* and unvoiced *th* }	puffs ducks maps cats myths
z	after	{ *b, d, g, ge, h, l, m, n, ng, q, r, v, w,* *y,* voiced *th,* and long vowels }	cobs lids gags judges pills hams vans cars lives bellows lathes flies
z		{ at the end of some one-syllable words. }	as has was is his
z		{ when the *s* occurs between two vowels }	arise closet miser

S IS SPELLED			
es	after	{ *j, s, x, z, ch, sh, zh* (after *y,* change the *y* to *i* and add *es*) *ladies* }	dresses boxes inches dishes fizzes flies
The *e* in *es* is silent		{ in the third person singular }	goes hoes
		{ in the plural of words except after sibilants }	stones horses

An exercise like the following helps the pupil to discriminate between the *s* and *z* sounds:

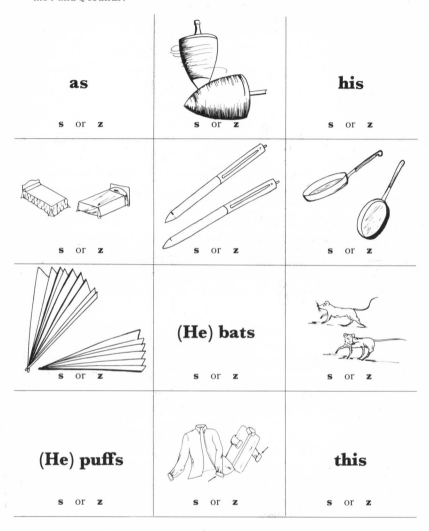

as		his
s or **z**	s or **z**	s or **z**
s or **z**	s or **z**	s or **z**
	(He) bats	
s or **z**	s or **z**	s or **z**
(He) puffs		**this**
s or **z**	s or **z**	s or **z**

Teaching the Compounds

The pupil may be introduced to two-syllable words through simple compounds. The pupil needs to learn that one-syllable words have only one vowel sound and that compounds each have two vowels that are sounded and therefore are called two-syllable words. He probably needs to learn this inductively. Burmeister[13] found that when the vowel is a vowel combination (*ai, oa*), the generalization "Every vowel combination means a syllable" was correct 85 per cent of the time.

A syllable is that part of a word which contains a vowel and which receives some stress. The syllable is very helpful in attacking new words. After all, monosyllabic words are merely syllables to which we have given a meaning. Hildreth[32] notes that "The syllable, not the phoneme, is the basic unit of speech articulation. . . ." There are two kinds of syllabication: one for writing and one for pronunciation. The former is inconsistent and generally one must consult the dictionary to be certain.

There are numerous simple compounds that are teachable at the primary level.

bedbug	cobweb	hamlet	onset	tidbit
bellhop	cutup	hellcat	pell-mell	tiptop
bigtop	dishpan	hubbub	pigpen	tomcat
bigwig	forbid	humbug	popgun	tomtom
bulldog	forget	into	sunlit	upon
carhop	godson	mudsill	sunset	upset
cannot	gunman	offset	sunup	wigwag

On more advanced levels the pupil should learn more difficult words, beginning with those compounds that keep the basic meaning of each word making up the compound. For example, a classroom is a room where class is held. Other words useful in teaching this skill are *byways, breakdown, campfire, cornstalk, cowboy, earthquake, eyelash, hillside, hilltop, limestone, railroad, rosebush, watchman, weekend, steamboat, workbook, snowshoes, sawdust, sandhill,* and *newsboy.*

Frequently, the meaning of the compound is completely new (broadcast, township, wholesale). Some compounds are written as two words (ice cream, living room, dining room, sea power, post office, oil painting, air brake, parcel post, money order, school spirit).

Whenever a compound word is used as a modifier and occurs before the word that it modifies, it is hyphenated. We speak of living-room furniture and a high-school dance. The hyphen also is used with self (self-denial, self-confidence, self-control) and with compound numbers from twenty-one to ninety-nine (twenty-six men). Here is a list of additional compounds:

airplane	eyebrow	nighttime	sundown
backbone	eyelash	northwest	sunset
bagpipe	farmland	outgrow	sunshade
barnyard	fireman	outline	sunshine
baseball	fishhook	outskirts	sunstroke
bedside	foreman	pancake	sunup
bedtime	footprint	plaything	tadpole
beehive	footstep	playtime	toothbrush
beeline	footstool	quicksand	touchdown
blacktop	grandstand	railroad	township
bobcat	grapevine	rainbow	trailways
bobsled	graveyard	ransack	treetop
bobwhite	gumdrop	roommate	upkeep
boldface	halfway	rosebush	uplift
bloodshed	hedgerow	sandhill	upset
boxcar	himself	sawdust	vineyard
broadcast	hillside	seacoast	warehouse
broomstick	hilltop	schoolroom	watchman
breakdown	horseback	seesaw	waylay
byways	inland	shipshape	weekend
campfire	inside	sideline	wholesale
cardboard	instep	sidetrack	wigwag
childhood	itself	signpost	wishbone
classmate	kidnap	smokestack	withdraw
classroom	limestone	snowshoes	within
corkscrew	lookout	soapsuds	without
cornstalk	makeshift	stagecoach	withstand
cowboy	mankind	starfish	windshield
daylight	maybe	statehood	woodpile
dragnet	milkman	steamboat	woodland
drumstick	milkshake	subway	workbook
earthquake	milkweed	sunburn	yardstick
elsewhere	newsboy	sunburst	yearbook
		Sunday	yuletide

Compounds may be taught in many ways.

1. An exercise like the following is simple, yet it emphasizes the use of the pupil's phonetic skills while the same time teaching syllabication.

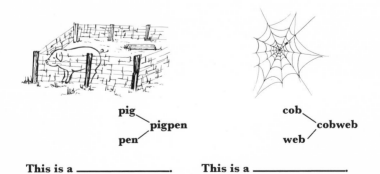

This is a _____.   This is a _____.

In the following exercise, the pupil needs to learn that only one of the double consonants is pronounced:

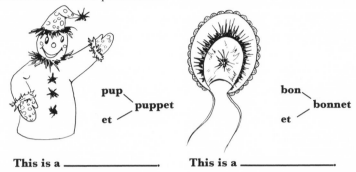

pup
et
puppet

bon
et
bonnet

This is a _____.   **This is a _____.**

2. Another technique for teaching the compounds is the following:

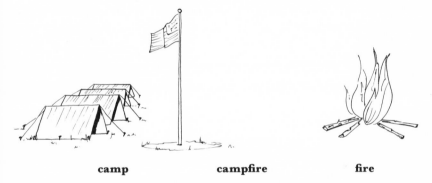

camp   **campfire**   **fire**

3. A third exercise consists of two columns of monosyllabic words found in compound words. The pupil is required to join a word in column I to a word in column II to form a compound word.

I	II	Compound Word
1. bell	1. top	1. bellhop
2. big	2. set	
3. sun	3. dog	
4. for	4. hop	
5. bull	5. get	

4. A fourth exercise consists of a page full of pictures. Each pair of pictures represents a compound word. Initially the pupil may be required only to pronounce the compound word. Later he may have to write the word.

fishhook

Teaching *ing*

After dealing with simple compounds, the pupil is ready to learn the ending *ing*. The teacher demonstrates how *ing* can be added to verbs to form two-syllable words (hitting, batting, getting, hopping, running, tagging, tugging, nagging, winning). The pupil should note that the consonant is doubled before adding the *ing* and that the second consonant is silent. Emans[24] reports that his rule has a 91 per cent utility. Bailey[3] found it had 98 per cent utility.
Exercises such as the following teach the use of *ing*:

Tom digs.
Tom is
digging.

Tom and
Pam hug.
Tom and Pam

are hug____.

She pets
her dog. She

is _____

her dog.

Tip gets the
ball. Tip is

_____

the ball.

After the pupil can deal successfully with long vowels in various combinations and after he has mastered the regular uses of *ing* as discussed above, he needs to expand his uses for *ing*. Whenever *ing* is added to monosyllabic words ending in a vowel, diphthong, or double vowel (being, playing, fleeing, hoeing), to monosyllabic words ending in a single consonant preceded by a double vowel (aiding), to monosyllabic words ending in a double consonant (arming), or to words ending in *ow* (blowing), no doubling of the letter preceding *ing* occurs. Monosyllabic words ending in a silent *e* drop the final *e* before adding *ing* (bake—baking). The first vowel receives its long sound in reading.

The principles suggested apply not only to *ing* but also to any suffix beginning with a vowel. The most common such suffixes are *able, ably, ability, age, ance, ant, ard, ary, ation, ed, en, ence, ent, er, ern ery, es, est, ion, ish, ity, ive, or, ous,* and *y*. Words ending in *ce* or *ge* retain the *e* before a suffix beginning with *a* or *o*.

The lists of words below illustrate these principles in all of their applications.

1. When *ing* is added to monosyllabic words ending in a vowel, diphthong, or double vowel and to words ending in *ow*, no doubling of the letter preceding the *ing* occurs.

being	flaying	freeing	growing
doing	playing	seeing	knowing
going	praying	hoeing	mowing
crying	saying	shoeing	rowing
flying	slaying	blowing	showing
frying	spraying	bowling	slowing
prying	staying	crowing	snowing
spying	straying	flowing	throwing
trying	fleeing	glowing	towing

2. When *ing* is added to monosyllabic words ending in a single consonant preceded by two vowels, no doubling of the letter preceding the *ing* occurs.

aiding	creeping	coasting	cleaning
claiming	feeding	floating	cheating
failing	feeling	loading	dreaming
nailing	keeping	roasting	leaking
painting	boasting	beating	bleeding

3. When *ing* is added to monosyllabic words ending in two consonants, no doubling of the consonant before *ing* occurs.

asking	drinking	hunting	singing
barking	dusting	kissing	fighting
bringing	falling	milking	holding
dressing	farming	missing	kicking
drilling	helping	rocking	pulling

4. When *ing* is added to monosyllabic words ending in a silent *e*, the *e* is dropped before adding *ing*.

baking	giving	praising
biting	hiding	smiling
coming	making	smoking
diving	moving	taking
driving		

The Past Tense with *ed*

The pupil also must be introduced to the past tense formed by *ed*. In reading *ed*, the child meets certain problems. The *e* is silent (begged, canned) except after *d* and *t* (batted, nodded). The *d* is pronounced as a *t* after the voiceless consonants such as *c*, *ch*, *f* (puffed), *h*, *k* (peeked), *p* (dipped), *s*, *sh* (wished), *t*, or *th*. The past participle of *dream*, *learn*, and *spell* may be pronounced with a *t* or a *d* sound.

The lists of words below exemplify these principles.

1. The *e* in *ed* is silent except after *d* and *t*.

batted	dusted	lasted	skidded
cheated	folded	nodded	started
dated	hated	planted	twisted
dotted	hunted	punted	waited
drifted	landed	scolded	wanted

2. The *d* is pronounced as a *t* after soft *c*, *ch*, *f*, *h*, *k*, *p*, *s*, *sh*, *t*, and *th*.

clapped	asked	huffed	dressed
helped	baked	puffed	kissed
hoped	barked	stuffed	missed
ripped	kicked	lunched	passed
roped	talked	preached	wished

An exercise such as the following develops skill in the use of *ed*. Have the pupils indicate whether the *ed* ending is pronounced *t*, *d*, or *ed*.

a. The dog be*gg*ed (begd) for a catfish.
b. The cop na*bb*ed (nabd) the gunman.
c. She no*dd*ed (nod-ed) to the man.
d. He pe*tt*ed (pet-ed) his wet cub.
e. She na*pp*ed (napt) on her bed.

Check the correct pronunciation of *ed*.

	d		d		d
nabbed	ed	mopped	ed	batted	ed
	t		t		t

	d		d		d
gagged	ed	nipped	ed	tipped	ed
	t		t		t

	d		d		d
wanted	ed	rubbed	ed	dotted	ed
	t		t		t

Roots, Prefixes, and Suffixes

Being able to break a word into its root, prefix, and suffix is a valuable skill in developing meaning for a word. This, however, is not enough. The pupil also must know the meaning of *root*, *prefix*, and *suffix*.

In teaching the pupil the structural skill here indicated, the teacher must follow definite steps. He must show the pupil that most two- and three-syllable words are composed of a root, a prefix, and/or a suffix. He next develops meaning for the words *root*, *prefix*, and *suffix*.

The root is the main part of a word. It is the reservoir of meaning. The prefix is that something which is put before the main part of a word or that which is put at the beginning of a word. The word *prefix* is composed of a root and a prefix. It comes from the Latin root *figere*, meaning to put or fix, and the Latin prefix *prae*, meaning before or at the beginning of.

The teacher should demonstrate to the pupil that prefixes change the meaning of a word, much as an adjective changes the meaning of a noun. In the sentence "The test was very difficult," the word *difficult* is an adjective, and it changes the meaning of the word *test*. The test could have been described as easy. Prefixes work in a similar way. Circumnavigate is composed of the prefix *circum* and the root *navigare*. *Navigare* is a Latin word meaning to sail. The prefix *circum* means around, and the entire word, *circumnavigate*, means to sail around. The prefix *circum* thus changes the meaning of the root by indicating that in this instance *navigare* is not just sailing, but is actually a particular type of sailing.

The suffix is another part of many two- or three-syllable words. It comes at the end of the word. It comes from the Latin words *sub* and *figere*, meaning to add on. The suffix frequently indicates the part of speech of the word. Thus, *ly* in *badly* is a suffix and usually indicates that the word is an adverb. The *ion* in *condition* is a suffix and usually indicates that the word is a noun.

Four combinations of root, prefix, and suffix are immediately indicated:

1. Root by itself, as in *stand*.
2. Prefix + root, as in *prefix*.
3. Root + suffix, as in *badly*.
4. Prefix + root + suffix, as in *insisting*.

Finally the pupil may be taught that when two roots are combined to form a word, the word is termed a compound word.

Studies have shown that a few Latin and Greek roots are very helpful in deciphering the meanings of thousands of words. Approximately twenty prefixes account for something like 85 per cent of the prefixes used in words. There also are some key suffixes.

Here is a list of twenty common Latin roots.

Infinitive	Meaning	Examples
agere, ago, egi, actum	to act, do, arouse, to set in motion, drive, transact, sue	agent, act, action, actuality, actual, active, actor
capere, capio, cessi, cessum	to give ground, to yield, to seize	seceded, cede, secession
ducere, duco, duxi, ductum	lead	duct, conduct, ductile, abduct, seduce
facere, facio, feci, factum	to do, make	fact, factory, benefit, factor, fashion, factual
	bear, carry	ferry, oblation, tolerate, ferret,
ferre, fero, tuli, latum		tolerant, toleration, transfer
legere, lego, legi, lectum	choose, collect, gather, read	elect, reelect, select, lector, lecturer, legendary
mittere, mitto, misi, missum	send	emit, mission, remit, submit, admit, missive
movere, moveo, movi, motum	move, arouse, excite	move, mobility, movable, movement, mover, movie
plicare (complicare), complico, complicavi, complicatum	to fold, confuse	complicate, duplicate, plicate, complication
ponere, pono, posui, positum	put, place	pose, opposite, post, position
portare, porto, portavi, portatum	carry	comport, port, export, import, report
regere, rego, rexi, rectum	to rule, guide, direct	direct, regular, rector, rectory, rex
scribere, scribo, scripsi, scriptum	to write	script, transcript, manuscript, inscription
specere, specio, spexi, spectum	to see	specious, specter, spectre, inspect
stare, sto, steti, statum	to stand, remain, endure	statue, insist, stationary, station
tenere, teneo, tenui, tentum	hold, have	tenuto, tenet, tenor, tenaculum
tendere, tendo, tentendi, tentum (tensum)	stretch out, extend, march toward	tend, tendency, tension, tender
venire, venio, veni, ventum	to come	event, convene, convention
videre, video, vidi, visum	to see	view, vision, visible, visit

Greek roots also are helpful in arriving at the meanings of words. Here are some Greek roots, of which the first two are by far the most common.

graphein–grapho, gegrapha	to write, inscribe	graph, phonograph, monograph, graphic
legein, lego	to tell, to say	(see *logos*)
aer	air, atmosphere	aerodynamics, aerate
autos	self	automatic, automobile
bios	life	autobiography, biography
geos	earth, land	geologist, geometry
heteros	other	heterodox, heterogeneity
homoios	like, same	homogeneity, homogenous
logos	word, thought, study of	geology, biology
micros	small	microscope, microcosm
monos	alone, only, once, one	monochord, monochrome
philos	friend	Philadelphia, philanthropy
phone	sound, tone, voice	telephone, phonic

physis	nature	physics, physical
polys	many	polygamy, polygamist
pseudos	lie, false	pseudonym, pseudoclassic
psyche	breath, life, spirit	psychometry, psychopath
sophos	wise, clever	philosopher, philosophy
telos	end	telephone, telegraph
tele	far	television

The pupil will learn to use roots in figuring out the meaning of words through an exercise similar to the following.

Here is a list of nine roots: *act* (to act), *capt* (to seize), *duct* (to lead), *mov* (to move), *port* (to carry), *script* (to write), *vis* (to see), *graph* (to write), and *auto* (by itself). Look now at the series of words below and identify the root that is used in each of the three words. Write the meaning of each of the words, using the dictionary when necessary.

1. active, actor, action, act.
   a. quality of being active, busy, energetic.
   b. one who acts, a doer.
   c. an act, the process of acting.
2. captor, captive, captured.
3. abduct, ductile, deduct.
4. movable, movement, mover.
5. export, import, report
6. transcript, inscription, manuscript
7. visual, vision, visible
8. monograph, biography, graphic.
9. automobile, automatic, autobiography.

Twenty prefixes are used rather frequently. These can be taught early in the elementary school years.

ab, a	away from, from	*ad, a ap, at*	to, toward
be	by	*com, co, cor, con, col*	with
de	from		
epi	upon	*dis, di*	apart
in, en. im, em	in, into	*ex, e*	out of
inter	between	*in, ir, il*	not
non	not	*mis*	wrong
pre	before	*ob, op, of*	against
re	back	*pro*	in front of
trans	across	*sub*	under
		un	not

Of less importance are the following:

ante	before	*circum*	around
contra	against	*intra, intre*	inside, within
per	through	*post*	after
amphi (ambi)	around, on both sides	*super*	above
dia	through	*anti*	against
syn	together	*peri*	around

One of the best ways of helping the student to increase his vocabulary is to run the root word through the prefix assembly line:

intra		*ad*
inter		*ab*
in		*mis*
ex		*non*
epi		*ob*
dis		*per*
dia	Root word, *port*	*peri*
de		*post*
contra		*pre*
com		*pro*
circum		*re*
be		*sub*
anti		*super*
ante		*syn*
amphi		*trans*
		un

Running the root word *port* through this sequence suggests the following words: *comport, deport, export, import, report, transport, and support.*

Another exercise requires the pupil to work out the meaning of a word when the prefix and its meaning are given.

	Prefix	*Meaning of Prefix*	*Meaning of Word*
transport	*trans*	across	. . . .
deduct	*de*	from, away from	. . . .
import	*in*	into	. . . .
subscript	*sub*	under	. . . .
invisible	*in*	not	. . . .
inactive	*in*	not	. . . .
unable	*un*	not	. . . .
adduce	*ad*	to, toward	. . . .
compose	*com*	with	. . . .
export	*ex*	out of	. . . .

A third exercise requires the pupil to identify the word when the meaning and the prefix are given.

to send out of the country (ex) . . . . export
to send into the country (in) . . . .
to turn a pupil away from school (ex) . . . .

There also are many suffixes that are helpful in working out the meanings of words. The pupil early learns to deal with *est, ing, er, or, ed,* and *d.* The following are other common suffixes:

Prefix	Meaning of Prefix	Meaning of Word
able, ible	capable of, worthy	durable, credible
age	act or state of	bondage, dotage
acy	quality of	lunacy, piracy
al, eal, ial	on account of, related to	judicial, terminal
ance, ence, ancy, ency	act or fact of doing, quality, state of	violence, temperance
ant	quality of one who	reliant, truant
ar, er, or	agent	scholar, author
dom	state, condition, fact of being	wisdom, kingdom
en	made of, to make	woolen, strengthen
eur	one who	amateur
ful	full of	graceful, blissful
fy	to make	falsify
ible, ile	capable of being	legible, docile
ier	one who	carrier
ic, ac	like, made of	maniac, metallic
ism	fact of being	barbarism
ity, ty	state of	unity, ability
ize	to put to, to make	memorize, modernize
less	without	motionless
let, et	small	cornet, hamlet
ly	like, characteristic	ably
ment	state or quality or act of doing	accomplishment
ness	state of	blindness
ous, ious, eous	abounding in, full of	joyous, courteous
tion, sion, xion	action, state of being, result	condition, tension
ty	quality or state of	liberty
ward	toward	southward

Exercises like the following develop the pupil's knowledge of the suffixes.

1. Using the list of suffixes and the meanings provided, select the word that says the same thing as the underlined words in each of the following sentences.

.... 1. The dog was <u>watching</u> the child carefully lest he wander onto the street
      a. watchful
      b. watcher

.... 2. The sky was <u>without a cloud.</u>
      a. cloudless
      b. cloudy

.... 3. The man <u>did not move a muscle.</u> He waited for the judge's verdict.
      a. movable
      b. motionless

.... 4. Are you <u>the man who will help me</u> with the job?
      a. helpful
      b. helper

.... 5. The United States is constantly forced to <u>bring</u> its armed forces <u>up to modern standards.</u>
      a. modern
      b. modernize

2. On the left side of the page may be written such simple questions as which is the tallest? Which is the fastest? Which is the hottest? The pupil puts an X through the picture that answers the question.

Which is the tallest?

Which is the fastest?

The Possessive Case and Contractions

The possessive case needs to be introduced to the pupil in the primary grades. The teacher must illustrate the use of the possessive and the apostrophe and must develop exercises that elicit from the pupil the correct application of the possessive rule.

The apostrophe is used also with contractions: *don't* (do not), *let's* (let us), *hasn't* (has not), *didn't* (did not), *can't* (can not), *I'm* (I am), *I'll* (I will), *I've* (I have), *haven't* (have not), *hadn't* (had not), *isn't* (is not), *wasn't* (was not), *he's* (he is), *he'll* (he will), *she's* (she is), *she'll* (she will), *you're* (you are), *you'll* (you will), *we're* (we are), *we'll* (we shall), *they're* (they are), *they'll* (they will).

In this instance the apostrophe indicates that one or more letters have been omitted.

An exercise similar to the following, requiring the pupil to match appropriate pairs, may be used to teach simple contractions on the first- and second-grade level.

does not	wasn't
can not	hasn't
will not	doesn't
was not	won't
has not	can't

Syllabication

Up to this point we have not emphasized the principles that govern accentuation and syllabication. Glass[27] questions the value of syllabication. He notes that usually the syllabication is done after the sounds in words become known. No one in Glass's study seemed to use syllabication rules to discover the sounds in words; rather, the sounds were used to determine syllable division. Glass adds, "Word analysis is not needed once the sound of the word is known" and asks, "Why syllabicate?" Schnell[49] raises the same question. Glass concludes that he can discover no reason why syllabication activities should be included in a word-analysis program.

At any rate, the good reader knows how to divide words accurately and rapidly. This does not mean that he divides every word that he comes to in his reading or that he knows the rule for dividing it. The former would slow down his reading and might even interfere with good comprehension. The latter is not necessary for good reading.

The first principle to be learned is that every syllable contains a sounded vowel. At times, a vowel itself constitutes a syllable: *a-corn*, *I*, *vi-o-let*, *lin-e-al*, *ce-re-al*, *o-pen*, *i-de-a*. A syllable thus is defined as a unit of pronounciation consisting of a vowel sound alone repetitious or with one or more consonant sounds and pronounced with one impulse.

The pupil also must learn that a syllable may contain more than one vowel. The number of syllables a word has is dependent upon the number of vowels heard, not by the number of vowels seen.

There are two kinds of syllables: closed syllables and open syllables. A closed syllable is one that ends with a consonant (cat, basis, magnetic). The vowel in a closed syllable is usually a short vowel. There are some common exceptions. These were discussed previously in this chapter under the heading "Principle of Position."

An open syllable is one that ends in a vowel (cry, by). The vowel in an open syllable is usually a long vowel. At one time the *y* at the end of a word often was pronounced as a short *i*; today, it is a long *e*. Below is a list of words with the *y* pronounced as long *e*.

ably	berry	cabby	copy	foggy	grassy
army	body	candy	crabby	folly	gravy
baby	brandy	carry	cranky	fifty	greasy
badly	buddy	clammy	dimly	filly	greedy
baldy	buggy	classy	drafty	funny	grimy
barley	bumpy	clumsy	empty	froggy	grisly
belfry	bunny	cocky	entry	gladly	grumpy
belly	busy	collie	flaky	glory	gusty

handy	jumpy	manly	poppy	sentry	sultry
happy	Kenny	marry	pussy	silly	sunny
hardy	kidney	muddy	putty	simply	taffy
hasty	kindly	nasty	rally	singly	tally
hefty	kingly	nifty	Randy	sissy	tinny
Henry	kinky	nippy	ruddy	sloppy	tippy
hobby	kitty	pantry	rummy	smelly	tipsy
holy	lackey	pappy	rusty	snappy	Tommy
homely	lady	parley	sadly	soggy	twenty
humbly	lanky	party	Sally	sorry	ugly
hungry	lassie	penny	scabby	spotty	wiggly
jelly	lately	pigmy	scanty	study	windy
jiffy	lily	pity	Scotty	stiffy	
jolly	madly	plenty			

Rule I

When two consonants follow a vowel, as in *after, kitten, pencil, summer*, and *butter*, the word is divided between the two consonants, and the first syllable ends with the first consonant. In instances of this kind the second consonant is silent when the consonants are the same. Since the first vowel is followed by a consonant, it tends to be a short vowel.

The pupil must be shown that not all double consonants can be divided. Consonant blends and speech consonants fall into this category.

Rule II

When only one consonant or a digraph follows a vowel, as in *paper, bacon, prefer, begun*, and *reshape*, the word usually is divided after the first vowel and the consonant or consonant digraph begins the second syllable. The first vowel, in that it ends a syllable, is usually a long vowel (si/lent, no/mad, ba/sin, da/tum, mi/nus, to/tal, ha/zel, si/nus, fa/tal, ca/det).

Exceptions and Observations

1. Not all words follow the rule. For example, *planet, solid, robin, travel, study, record,* river, primer,* present,* cabin, tropic, power, timid, habit, pity, body, quiver, copy, lily, bigot, calico, atom, honor, venum, olive, legend, lemon, valid, limit, dragon, wagon, digit, solid,*

---

* These may be divided according to both rules, dependent upon their meaning in the sentence.

cherish, volume, lizard, snivel, cherub, and *profit* join the consonant to the first vowel. This makes the first vowel short and the accent is on the first syllable.

2. The suffix *ed* is a syllable only when it follows the sound *d* or *t*.

3. Whenever two or more consonants appear between two vowels, the pupil must learn to look for consonant blends or speech consonants. They are never divided (gam-bler, mi-grate).

4. Whenever *le* ends a word and is preceded by a consonant, the last syllable consists of the consonant and the *le* (ta-ble, mid-dle, peo-ple). When *le* is preceded by *ck*, *le* is a separate syllable (freck/le, buck/le). The *e* in *ble, the, ple,* and *dle* is silent. Some authors, however, suggest that *le* says *el* with *e* being shorter than usual and called *schwa.*

Observe that in *tle* the *t* sometimes is silent and at times may be pronounced. Thus in *battle, bottle, brittle, mantle, cattle, little, rattle,* and *tattle* the *t* is pronounced; in *castle, hustle, jostle,* and *rustle* (words in which *tle* follows the letter *s*), it is silent.

able	cradle	kettle	raffle	scuttle
ankle	dazzle	kindle	ramble	stable
apple	dimple	little	rattle	steeple
babble	double	mantle	riddle	struggle
battle	fable	maple	rifle	table
beetle	fondle	marble	ripple	tackle
Bible	fumble	mangle*	rubble	tangle*
bicycle	gable	meddle	ruffle	tattle
bobble	gamble	middle	rustle	temple
bottle	gargle	mingle*	saddle	tickle
brittle	gentle	muddle	sample	tingle*
bubble	giggle	muffle	scuffle	title
buckle	grumble	mumble	simple	trample
bugle	haggle	muscle	single*	trifle
bundle	handle	nimble	sizzle	triple
bungle*	humble	nibble	smuggle	treble
cable	hustle	nipple	sniffle	tremble
cackle	jiggle	paddle	snuggle	tumble
candle	jingle*	pebble	spangle*	turtle
castle	little	pickle	sparkle	twinkle
cattle	jostle	pimple	swindle	uncle
circle	juggle	puddle	stubble	waggle
coddle	jumble	purple	supple	wiggle
crackle	jungle*	puzzle	scuffle	wriggle
		rabble		

* when *gle* is preceded by *n*, it is pronounced as gg'l.

5. Sometimes it is necessary to divide between two vowels (cre-ate). Common words in which this occurs are the following:

ai—archaic, laity, mosaic
ea—cereal, create, delineate, fealty, ideal, laureate, lineate, linear, permeate
ei—being, deity, reinforce, reinstate, spontaneity
eu—museum, nucleus
ie—client, diet, dietary, expedient, orient, piety, propriety, quiet, science
oa—coadjutor, coagulate, oasis
oe—coefficient, coerce, coexist, poem
oi—egoist, going
oo—cooperate, coordinate, zoology
ue—cruel, duel, duet, fluent, fuel, gruel, influence, minuet
ui—altruism, ambiguity, annuity, fluid, fruition

6. In a compound word the division comes between the two words making up the compound (post-man).
7. Prefixes and suffixes are usually set apart from the rest of the word (in-sist, great-est).

Accentuation

A word of two or more syllables generally is pronounced with more stress on one syllable. This is termed *accent*. In most dictionaries the accent mark (′) is placed just after the syllable that receives major stress. In words of three or more syllables there may be a secondary accent (lo′co mo′tive).

The teaching of accentuation is usually put off until the pupil is well advanced in phonic analysis and word analysis generally. After the pupil has learned the meaning of accent and the way the dictionary identifies the accent or stress point, he may gradually be introduced to the following rules:

1. Generally, words of two syllables in which two consonants follow the first vowel accent the first syllable (after, kitten, puppet, butter). This rule has 81 per cent utility.[3]
2. When a two-syllable word contains two vowels in the second syllable but only one is pronounced, the second syllable generally is accented (abide, abode, above, about, aboard, delay, proceed). Usually, the last syllable is long.
3. Compound words usually carry the primary accent on or within the first word (bellhop, bulldog, carhop, dishpan, godson, humbug, superman, pigpen). There are many exceptions to this rule (forbid).

4. In three-syllable words in which the suffix is preceded by a single consonant (adviser, exciting, translated, refusal) or (piloted, traveling, shiver-
ing), the accent may be on the first or second syllable. It is on the first
syllable except when the root word (advise, excite, translate, and refuse)
ends in *e* and the last syllable is accented.

5. In general, the accent is placed on alternate syllables (dis'-ap-point'-
ment). Frequently, the accented syllable is followed by two unaccented
syllables (san'-i-ty). At times the accent is on alternate syllables and the
last two syllables are unaccented (op'-por-tun'-i-ty).

6. Root words when preceded by prefixes or followed by suffixes usually are
accented (amuse, amusement).

7. Words ending in *ion, ity, ic, ical, ian, ial,* or *ious* have the accent immediately before these suffixes (consternation, athletic, immersion, industrial,
harmonious, humidity, psychological, historian). This rule is valid 95
per cent of the time.[24]

8. Words of three or more syllables ending in a silent *e* usually accent the
third from the end (graduate, accommodate, anticipate).

9. Homographs, words with identical spellings, receive their accent from
the context in which they are used (con'tract, contract').

In introducing the pupil to accent and syllabication, the teacher
needs to use words that the pupil knows. Repeated exercise with
actual words will help the pupil to obtain a functional knowledge
of the generalizations stated above.

Initially the teacher may pronounce a word orally and may let
the pupils indicate by one or two fingers whether the word has one
or two syllables or whether the accent falls on the first or second syllable. Gradually, the pupil should learn to write a word, divide it,
indicate its accent, and at the upper-grade levels may give the rules
which govern its syllabication and accentuation.

Summary

This chapter might have been put earlier in the sequence. It deals
with skills of analysis that the pupil should learn quite early, but since
we are interested in completeness, it also contains a discussion of skills
whose teaching must be deferred until the pupil has become a rather
proficient reader. It is our hope that the teacher, using this manual,
will teach some of the content early in the first grade and will delay
the introduction of other skills until the pupil has become quite
skilled in the application of phonic knowledge.

IX

MISCELLANEA

In this chapter we concern ourselves with more advanced but important skills. They are miscellanea only in that the content of each section of the chapter does not relate as closely to each preceding or subsequent section as does the content of earlier chapters. Perhaps, it is beneficial to list the content here.

1. Silent Letters
2. Common Sight Words
3. Homonyms
4. Problems of Multisyllabic Words
5. Principles of Teaching

Silent Letters

Sometime in his reading education the pupil should learn that certain consonants are not pronounced. When this situation prevails, the word frequently needs to be taught as a sight word. There are, however, some observations that apply consistently. For example, when a consonant is doubled, the first often is silent: *hitting*. The following are other examples where a consonant is silent:

Silent *b* after *m*:	bomb, comb, bomber, bombproof, bombshell, climb, crumb, dumb, lamb, limb, numb, plumb, plumber, plumbing, succumb, thumb, tomb, womb.
Silent *b* before all consonants, except *l* and *r*:	debt, debtor, doubt, doubtful, subtle, blend, double, breath.
Silent *c*:	czar, indict, victuals, sack, back, neck, block, kick, duck, clock, black, trick, back, pick.
Silent *ch*:	drachm, fuchsia, schism, yacht.
Silent *c* after *s*:	ascend, ascent, descend, descent, scene, scenic, scent, scepter, muscle, science, scissor, transcend.
Silent *d*:	adjunct, adjust, handerchief, handsome, Wednesday.
Silent *d* before *g*:	badger, dodger, edge, fudge.

126

Silent *g* before *n :*	align, arraign, benign, campaign, design, ensign, feign, foreign, gnarl, gnash, gnat, gnaw, gnome, malign, reign, resign, sign, signer, signpost.
Silent *gh :*	sigh, light, sight, bright, flight, night, might, slight, blight, right, eight, freight, neigh, neighbor, sleigh, straight, straighten, weigh, weight. Bailey[3] found that *gh :* is silent 100 per cent of the time when it precedes *t.*
Silent *h :*	aghast, ah, diarrhea, Durham, exhaust, exhibit, forehead, ghost, heir, hemorrhage, honest, honestly, honor, hour, hourly, khan, khaki, myrrh, oh, rhesus, rhetoric, rhinestone, rhinoceros, rhubarb, rhumb, rhyme, rhythm, rhythmic, shepherd, Thomas, Thomism, Thompson, vehement, vehicle.
Silent *k* before *n :*	knack, knap, knapsack, knave, knead, knee, kneel, knelt, knew, knife, knight, knit, knob, knock, knoll, knot, know, knowledge, knuckle, This observation has 100 per cent utility.[3] The silent *k* at times helps to distinguish between homonyms (new—knew; night—knight).
Silent *l :*	almond, alms, balk, balmy, behalf, calf, calk, calm, chalk, embalm, folk, folklore, half, jaywalk, kinsfolk, palm, polka, psalm, salmon, solder, talk, walk, would, yolk.
Silent *n* after *m :*	autumn, column, condemn, damn, damned, hymnal, solemn, solemnly.
Silent *p :*	corps, cupboard, pneumatic, pneumonia, psalm, psalmist, psalter, pseudo, psyche, psychiatry, psychic, psychology, raspberry, receipt.
Silent *s :*	aisle, Arkansas, bas-relief, Carlisle, chamois, corps, debris, Illinois, island, isle, Louisville, rendezvous, St. Louis, viscount.
Silent *t :*	bustle, castle, chasten, chestnut, Christmas, fasten, hasten, hautboy, hustle, listen, Matthew, mortgage, mustn't, often, soften, thistle, whistle, *t* is silent also when it precedes *ch* in the same syllable (catch, latch).
Silent *th :*	asthma
Silent *w :*	awry, answer, boatswain, bowler, enwrap, own, owner, rewrite, sword, swordfish, swordsman, toward, two, who, whole, wholeness, wholesale, wholesome, wholly, whom, whose, wrack, wraith, wrangle, wrangler, wrapper, wrath, wreak, wreath, wreck, wreckage, wren, wrench, wrest, wrestle, wrestling, wretch, wring, wrinkle, wrist, wristband, writ, write, writer, writing, writhe,

wrong, wrongly, wrote, wroth, wrought, wrung, wry, and often in the ending *ow* as in show. The *w* is always silent before *r*.[3]

Common Sight Words

There are many words that the pupil has to learn as sight words.

above	choir	full	many	some	two
again	come	get	move	someone	walk
against	coming	girl	Mr.	something	wand
aisle	cough	give	Mrs.	sometime	want
already	country	glove	none	son	war
always	cousin	goes	of	steak	was
another	cover	gone	off	sugar	wash
answer	do	half	often	sure	wasp
anxious	dog	has	once	swap	were
any	does	have	one	swat	what
are	done	heart	only	talk	where
as	don't	hearth	own	the	who
aunt	double	his	other	there	whom
been	dove	hour	people	to	whose
blood	dozen	into	pretty	today	wind
both	eight	is	pull	together	wolf
break	enough	isle	push	ton	women
bull	eye	know	put	too	won
bury	flood	laugh	rough	touch	won't
busy	four	leopard	said	tough	write
business	friend	live	says	tour	you
buy	from	log	sew	toward	young
canoe	front	love	shoes	trouble	your

Homonyms

Homonyms are words that are sounded alike but that have different spellings and meaning. They frequently lead to recognition and meaning difficulties. To illustrate their difference in the early grades the teacher must use them in meaningful context. Thus, the difference between *blue* and *blew* is brought out in the following sentences:

1. The wind blew down the house.
2. Mary wore a blue dress.

Following is a list of some common homonyms:

ate–eight	berth–birth	course–coarse	flee–flea
base–bass	blue–blew	dear–deer	flower–flour
be–bee	bow–bough	do–dew	forth–fourth
bear–bare	break–brake	fair–fare	four–for
beat–beet	buy–by	fir–fur	hair–hare

haul–hall	owe–oh	sea–see	vane–vein–vain
heel–heal	pain–pane	seen–scene	wade–weighed
here–hear	pair–pare	sew–so	waist–waste
hour–our	peace–piece	sight–site–cite	wait–weight
made–maid	plane–plain	some–sum	wave–waive
mail–male	principal–principle	steak–stake	way–weigh
meet–meat	rain–rein	steal–steel	week–weak
new–knew	rap–wrap	sun–son	whole–hole
night–knight	read–reed	tail–tale	wood–would
no–know	read–red	their–there	write–right
not–knot	road–rode	through–threw	wrote–rote
one–won	sail–sale	to–too–two	

Problems of Multisyllabic Words

Appendix IV lists numerous two-syllable words for teaching and illustrating the principles and generalizations taught in previous chapters. Here we are more concerned with the special problems that multisyllabic words introduce.

Multisyllabic words introduce numerous problems not usually met in one-syllable words. For example, in one-syllable words one expects a long middle vowel when the word ends in a silent *e* (dame, dine, plume). This rule does not apply in some multisyllabic words.

ace = əs: solace, furnace, Horace, menace, palace, preface, surface.

age = ij: adage, baggage, bandage, bondage, breakage, cabbage, carnage, carriage, cleavage, coinage, cottage, courage, damage, dosage, drainage, forage, garbage, homage, hostage, image, language, leakage, luggage, manage, marriage, message, mileage, mortgage, orphanage, package, passage, pillage, postage, pottage, roughage, rummage, salvage, sausage, savage, scrimmage, sewage, seepage, soilage, soakage, spoilage, village, vintage, voltage, voyage, wastage, wattage, wreckage, yardage.

ege = ēg: renege.

ege = ej: college.

ege = ij: privilege.

ige = ēzh: prestige.

ase = əs: purchase.

ate = ət: chocolate, climate, deliberate, delicate, delegate, desolate, duplicate, frigate, palate, prelate, private, senate, separate, temperate.

ice = əs: chalice, complice, crevice, justice, malice, notice, novice, office, practice, service.

ice = ēs: caprice, police.

ile = *il:*	agile, docile, fertile, fragile, futile, hostile, missile, mobile, repitle, servile, sterile, tractile, virile.*
ile = *ēl:*	automobile, castile.
ine = *in:*	doctrine, engine, ermine, famine, genuine, urine, but also long *i* as in divine, turpentine.
ine = *ēn:*	carbine, machine, marine, morphine, ravine, routine, sardine, vaccine.
ise = *əs:*	premise, promise, treatise.
ise = *ēs:*	valise.
ite = *ət:*	respite.
live = *iv:*	active, captive, festive, massive, motive, passive, positive, native, detective, talkative, locomotive, destructive, adjective, attentive, objective, elective, sensitive, protective, executive, relative, attractive, creative, selective.
ive = *ēv:*	naive.
uce = *əs:*	lettuce.

The following are examples of other problems in reading multisyllabic words.

ain = *ən:*	bargain, Britain, captain, certain, chaplain, chieftain, curtain, fountain, mountain, villain.
ay = *ē:*	Monday, yesterday.
ia = *i:*	marriage, parliament.
ience = *shens:*	patience.
ce, ci, si, ti, as *sh:*	ocean; electrician, musician, physician, politician, cordial, social, racial, special, facial, glacial, official, special; ancient, sufficient, efficient; precious, spacious, delicious, conscious, ferocious, cautious, gracious, spacious, vicious; mission, cession, decision, fusion, lesion, occasion, passion, pension, tension, torsion, version; action, attention, auction, caption, caution, definition, diction, edition, faction, fraction, friction, function, junction, ignition, lotion, mention, motion, nation, notion, option, portion, potion, sanction, section, station, traction, unction, partial, martial, nuptial, confidential, residential, potential, tertian, patient, patience, quotient, transient, ambitious, militia.
s = *sh:*	mansion, nauseous, issue, tissue.
s = *zh:*	vision, visual, usury, fusion.

---

* chief exception is *gentile;* also note *exile, crocodile, reconcile, juvenile, infantile, mercantile,* and *versatile* have both pronunciations.

sure = chər, zhər:	censure, measure, pleasure, pressure, tresure, tonsure,
i = y:	familiar, peculiar, genius, behavior, junior, senior, guardian, brilliant, Italian, valiant, billion, companion, million, onion, opinion, union, Spaniard, spaniel, congenial, convenience, convenient, Daniel, William, Julia, California, Virginia, Pennsylvania, Celia, Philadelphia.
i = long ē:	broccoli, ski, spaghetti, police, machine, antique, physique, technique, unique, clique, pique, intrigue, fatigue.
du + r = jər:	procedure, verdure; exceptions: endure.
tu + r = chər:	capture, creature, culture, departure, feature, fracture, furniture, future, fixture, gesture, lecture, mixture, nature, pasture, picture, puncture, stature, suture, tincture, texture, torture, venture, vulture; mature is an exception.
tu + any other letter *= chə:*	actual, mutual, virtuous.
zure = zhər	seizure, azure.
ous = əs	dangerous, curious, enormous, courteous, previous, nervous, prosperous, poisonous, furious, generous, studious, numerous, mysterious, tedious, continuous.

Principles of Teaching and Learning

In closing this chapter perhaps a few summarizing statements that should guide teaching are apropos.

1. Teachers need to be aware that sometimes the pupil comes up with the correct response by accident or by guessing, *without understanding why his answer is correct.*
2. The teacher needs to determine whether to reward the correct response, the correct process, or only the correct response when it is accompanied by the correct process.
3. The pupil learns by doing; learning occurs under conditions of practice, and overlearning is of crucial importance to poor readers. Children generally become better in word recognition the more frequently they see the word. However, practice or repetition per se does not cause learning. The pupil's practice must be both motivated and rewarded, and it should be slightly varied from session to session.
4. The learner learns best when he is psychologically and physiologically ready to respond to the stimulus. The learner needs a proper attitude, should be ready to attend to the stimulus, and should have a felt need to learn. He needs also to have adequate maturity for learning. The learner will not respond unless he is motivated, and he cannot learn unless he responds. The reader's performance will improve only if he is interested

in his work, if he is interested in improving himself, if the material to be learned has special significance for himself, and if he is attentive to the situation. Reduce motivations to zero and there is no performance and, hence, no learning.

5. The learner cannot learn without doing, but he will not do anything without being rewarded. The best rewards in the reading setting are often pleasant pupil-teacher relationships, permissiveness on the part of the teacher, and feelings of success. The teacher must divide the learning situation into numerous small steps and must reward the learning of each discrete step.

6. Learning is often a matter of present organization and reorganization, not simply past accretion. Perhaps, no individual is ever completely free to behave on the basis of the present situation. Previous experiences have developed a set or pattern of behavior that is difficult to change. The retarded reader, even if he now sincerely wants to be a good reader, must live with his previous inapplications, but, each new situation has within it the potentiality for change. The pupil can usually make positive advances toward new goals and achievements. He has the potentiality for growth.

7. Letters might best be taught to most children as parts of a whole word, but the perceptual whole for the retarded reader often is the single letter. The size of the unit of instruction depends on the nature of the pupil, and many retarded readers benefit greatly from a synthetic-phonetic approach.

8. The teacher needs to ask himself whether he is trying to get the pupil to substitute one stimulus for another or whether he wants to elicit the correct response. In teaching the child to read, we obviously have a case of stimulus substitution. In essence, we are asking the child to bring to the written word the same meanings that he previously attached to the spoken word.

Reading also involves response selection. A child who can read *the* and *there* may not be too sure of *their*. He makes provisional tries at the word and when he comes up with the correct pronunciational response the teacher reinforces this response, thus gradually stamping it in. Thus, from a series of possible responses the pupil gradually learns to select the correct response.

9. Each activity (reading of a sentence, for example) consists of a complex of individual movements, and improvement and learning are not necessarily attained by *much* reading but rather by increasing the number of correct movements in reading (moving from left to right, proper identification of the word, association of the proper meaning with the word, development of proper eye movements), and by reducing the number of incorrect movements (excessive regressions, improper word attack) in the total complex of movements comprising the total capacity. Improvement occurs because the learner gradually replaces the erro-

neous movements that he still is making with correct ones. Thus additional practice gives more opportunity to master the myriad of movements comprising a complex total performance.

This view of the learning of a skill certainly emphasizes the need for the teaching of specific habits. Telling a retarded reader "to read" is not specific enough. We need to teach specific habits in specific situations. This requires careful job analysis, leading to an identification of all specific movements. The curriculum, methods, and materials must be so specific that they will serve as proper stimuli to call forth appropriate.

It is not enough to identify large, all-embracing abilities such as "gaining a sight vocabulary." It is necessary to break the broad area into basic subskills such as the ability to discriminate between sounds or to see elements within a word.

10. It is important that the teacher not permit the learner to leave a learning situation without performing the response correctly. A pupil should read the word correctly before going on to another word.

    The reader should not "get by" with approximations of the correct answer.[11] The pupil should not be permitted simply to get a "general idea." Teachers frequently give partial credit for partially correct answers. Partially correct answers such as reading *their* for *them* are in fact totally wrong. Bugelski notes that "Too many students are rated as 'knowing what to do' without being able to do."

11. If the learner tends to repeat the response that was made most recently in the presence of the stimulus (Law of Relative Recency), the teacher should exercise great care, especially with the retarded reader, in not permitting extraneous materials to come between the stimulus and response. The teacher must see to it that when the response is made, it is made to the proper stimulus and not to any of many other possible stimuli that may have intervened. Too frequently, in teaching, by the time the proper response occurs, the original stimulus situation has disappeared. The teacher must take great care that the necessary stimuli are so distinct for the pupil so he cannot help but see the connection between a given stimulus and the objective of teaching.

12. Learning retardation frequently results because the pupil cannot make the proper differentiations required for mastery of the learning task.

    Differentiations take time and the teacher must constantly make adjustments for this. Thus the application of white paint at the choice points in an otherwise completely black maze leads to quicker and more accurate learning by the rat. In classroom learning, the method of teaching can be simplified or made unnecessarily difficult. The teacher can arrange the learning situation in such a way that the differentiations come easily or are more difficult. Teaching machines essentially strive to make each step to be learned so simple and small that it can be taken with great confidence and success. With the retarded reader, in particular, the learning task needs to be presented in structured, carefully planned steps.

The manner in which a problem is presented determines at least in some way whether past experiences can be used appropriately or not. Some classroom arrangements are more conducive than others to the elicitation of insightful solutions. The evidence indicates that with retarded readers, who often are weak in the visual-association–memory area, materials should be presented through the auditory and kinesthetic channels.

In *Diagnosis and Remediation of Reading Disability*, Parker Publishing Company, West Nyack, New York, 1968, we outlined specific principles for teaching the retarded reader and such specific cases of retardation as exhibited by the dyslexic reader, the reluctant reader, the slow learner, the experientially deprived child, and the emotionally disturbed child.

Summary

The initial phonic exercises should have one chief function: developing a reading vocabulary. This may be done in many ways. It is possible to form a direct association between meaning and the printed symbol. In this case the word is identified through its shape and configuration or through picture-reading. Another approach continues training in auditory and visual discrimination and involves phonetic and structural analysis. The child associates the whole word with a sound, but from the beginning identifies letters or groups of letters that recur repeatedly in words and that constantly have the same sound. These parts of words give clues to the sounds of other words, thus helping the child both to pronounce and indirectly to associate meaning with the printed symbol. This method starts with the initial consonant and teaches the child to read through the word. This means proceeding from left to right, much as in reading a sentence.

There is little research to indicate which words children should learn first. Present assumptions in this regard are based on frequency count. But is this a valid criterion? Word length may be a more important consideration than frequency of use. The longer the word, the more difficult it is. We believe that vocabulary control in the linguistic-phonics program should be based on the regularity of the grapheme-phoneme pattern; on phonetic difficulty, not semantic difficulty. We are concerned most with teaching those words that most aid in the acquisition of a vocabulary.

The materials in this book are in no way intended to constitute a reading program or to limit the child's reading. It is not necessary for each pupil to learn on the spot each new word that he encounters. The development of a recognition vocabulary should be based on (1) the acquisition of words that can only be learned by sight or configuration, (2) the acquaintance with numerous words that only gradually become a part of the pupil's reading vocabulary (no great emphasis should be put on these in early reading), and (3) the acquisition of a method that permits the pupil to work out the pronunciation of new words. This book has been concerned primarily with this last aspect.

X

MATERIALS FOR TEACHING LINGUISTIC AND PHONIC SKILLS

W<small>ITH</small> the vast array of materials available today, it is important that we have some guidelines so that we may choose and spend wisely. School districts need to get an effective return on every dollar spent.

There is no panacea for reading problems, but the newer media can help. It is most important that the materials used with a given pupil are suited to his needs. Incorrect materials or the incorrect use of appropriate materials can actually cause or intensify reading problems. In selecting materials, the teacher needs to make sure that they are on an appropriate interest level and that they take into account the pupil's deficiencies and problems. It makes sense to vary materials from time to time and to use in remedial instruction materials that are normally not used in the classroom.

It certainly behooves the teacher to proceed cautiously in the selection of materials. Today, with the great proliferation of phonetic alphabets, with claims that specific approaches can lead to the solution of all reading problems, with the obvious contradictions between methods and approaches, and with the press again popularizing a given approach as *the* solution, it is imperative that the teacher become extremely selective as he looks at the materials explosion.

We have organized the materials in this section by companies. It is hoped that the major phonic and linguistic programs are included in this survey.

1. *Happy Times with Sounds Series*, Allyn and Bacon, Inc.*
   This series consists of four books that give a complete course in phonics.
2. *Peabody Rebus Reading Program*, American Guidance Service, Inc., Circle Pines, Minnesota.

---

* For addresses of publishers, see Appendix V.

This is a programmed approach to readiness and beginning reading instruction.

It consists of two workbooks, using a vocabulary of picture words (rebuses).

3. *Listen and Learn with Phonics*, American Interstate Corporation.

This is a home course in phonics based on records and booklets, plus word and letter strips. The beginner's set is used with children up to and including second grade and consists of four illustrated booklets and three unbreakable records. An advanced set, the remedial set, is similar to the first, but contains only two records. Accompanying the sets are Funagrams, a domino-like game that uses cardboard strips with phonograms on one end and consonants and consonant blends on the other, and L&L Educational Game Set, an educational word-building game.

4. *Michigan Successive Discrimination Language Program*, Ann Arbor Publishers.

This programmed basal reading series covers auditory, visual, and space discrimination, letters, words, phrases, sentences, paragraphs, manuscript writing, phonemic analysis, spelling, oral composition, and comprehension.

5. *Beckley-Cardy Aids for Teaching Phonics*, Beckley-Cardy Company.

(1) *Phonics for Reading* (for slow readers)

(2) *Phonetic Word Wheel* (grades 2 and 3)

(3) *Learn to Read Workbooks*

These two workbooks—the first of which is for grades 1, 2, and 3 and the second of which is for grades 4 and above—provide a program in phonics.

(4) *Phonics Fun* (two workbooks for grades 1 and 2)

(5) *Building Words* (phonics workbook for grade 1)

(6) *Phonics Skilltexts* (phonics workbooks for grades 1 through 5)

6. *Hayes Mastery Phonics Workbooks*, Beckley-Cardy Company.

This series consists of six books that give a complete coverage of the phonic skills.

7. *Listen and Learn with Phonics Records*, Beckley-Cardy Company.

Four phonics books, three 78-rpm records, Turn-a-Wheel, and Word Chart are the materials in this program. The set is usable in conjunction with any primers and readers.

8. *Reading Preparation Books*, Beckley Cardy Company.

These two books develop left-to-right eye movements and motor coordination.

9. *Reading*. M. W. Sullivan, Behavioral Research Laboratories.

This is two-series program of eight books designed to develop basic alphabetic, phonic, and structural skills.

10. *Telezonia*, Bell Telephone Company.

Designed for grades 4–9 this unit includes telephones and fifty-one filmstrips. It teaches such reading skills as following directions and skimming.

11. *Cordts Phonetic Books*, Benefic Press.

Three books, *I Can Read, Hear me Read*, and *Reading's Easy*, make up this set for levels 1, 2, and 3.

12. *Functional Phonetics Worktexts*, Benefic Press.

This program is in harmony with the whole-word recognition or the look-say method of teaching reading. Instructs beginning readers in a technique for identifying an unfamiliar word in reading, and provides remedial reading procedures that improve speech and spelling at any level. Readiness level is 1, 2, and 3.

13. *Seatwork Books*, Benton Review Publishing Company.
    This series of five books is designed to develop a basic vocabulary. The books are entitled *Let's Get Started, Fun with Words and Pictures, Fun with Words— Grade I, Fun with Words—Grade II*, and *More Fun with Words—Grade III*.

14. *The Sound Way Series*, Benton Review Publishing Company.
    These two books develop the pupil's phonic skills.

15. *The Sound Way to Easy Reading*, Brenner-Davis Phonics, Inc.
    This consists of four records and fifteen wall charts.

16. *Ways to Read Words, More Ways to Read Words*, and *Learning About Words*, Bureau of Publications, Columbia University.
    These three books develop fundamental phonic skills usually taught in grades 2–4.

17. *Landon Phonics Program*, Chandler Publishing Company.
    This phonics program for kindergarten through grade 2 is designed to supplement basic reading series. The program consists of nineteen records (or tapes) and seventy-six worksheets.

18. *Building Reading Power*, Charles E. Merrill Books, Inc.
    This programmed course for improving reading techniques is designed for students who read on or about the fifth-grade level. There are fifteen different booklets, covering such topics as picture and verbal context, visual clues, definitions, synonyms, antonyms, context, prefixes, suffixes, main ideas, central thought of a paragraph, and details of a paragraph.

19. *New Phonics Skilltexts*, Charles E. Merrill Books, Inc.
    These texts develop phonic skills, structural-analysis skills, comprehension skills, and listening skills. The books range from grade 1–6. Book D, for grades 4–6, introduces speech sounds, presents sounds in context, develops the association between the sound and the letter, and illustrates the phonic principle.

20. *Linguistics Readers*, Charles E. Merrill Books, Inc.
    A series of readers which depends heavily on sound-symbol relationship.

21. *Iroquois Phonics Series*, Charles E. Merrill, Inc.

22. *Dialog I, An Aural-Oral Course in Phonics*, Chester Electronics Laboratories.
    These thirty-one tapes, accompanied by sixty-two booklets, provide a programmed phonics course for first grade or remedial groups.

23. *Reading Along With Me Series*, Teachers College, Columbia University.
    This series by Allen and Allen is a linguistic approach for teaching reading to preschool and primary-grade children. The child learns the shape of the letters, common spellings for sounds, and learns to read whole sentences. Included are *Story Booklet, Rhyming Words and Simple Sentences Booklet*, Alphabet Cards, and Anagram Cards.

24. *Continental Basic Reading Series*, Continental Press, Inc.
    This series, for grades 1 and 2, includes the following materials:

a. Reading Readiness Materials for Kindergarten and Grade One
   Rhyming, I and II
   Visual Motor Skills, I and II
   Beginning Sounds, I and II
   Independent Activities, I and *II*
   Thinking Skills, I and *II*
b. *We Get Ready to Read* . . . . preprimer
c. *We Get Ready to Read* . . . . primer
d. *We Learn to Read* . . . . grade 1
e. *We Learn to Read* . . . . grade 1
f. *ABC Book* . . . . grades 1 and 2
g. *Reading-Thinking Skills* . . . . grade 2

25. *Flight Through Wordland*, Continental Press, Inc.
    These thirty lessons for grade 4 deal with consonant digraphs and blends, long and short vowels, dictionary work, diacritical markings, syllables, prefixes, and suffixes. The lessons are available for duplication.
26. *Reading Thinking Skills*, Continental Press, Inc.
    This program, from preprimer level through grade 6, includes sixteen books for liquid duplicator. Certain skills common to higher-level thinking are treated at every level of the program. These include those concerned with word meaning, relationships, evaluation, inference, generalization, selection, and organization.
27. *Through Space to Wordland*, Continental Press, Inc.
    These thirty lessons on fifth-grade level, available for duplication, deal with the dictionary, word recognition, and word analysis.
28. *Wordland Series*, Continental Press.
    This is a complete phonics program for grades 1 through 5 with the following titles: *Fun in Wordland*, grade 1; *A Trip through Wordland*, grade 2; *Adventures in Wordland*, grade 3; *A Flight through Wordland*, grade 4, and *Through Space to Wordland*, grade 5.
29. *Coronet Films*, Coronet Films, Inc.

    1. "Fun with Speech Sounds"—covers the vowels and consonants *p*, *m*, *l*, *r*, *th*, and *ch* and is designed for the primary level.
    2. "Reading for Beginners: Word Sounds."
    3. "Do Words Ever Fool You?" —deals with listening development (intermediate level).
    4. "Listen Well, Learn Well"—deals with the problems of critical reading (intermediate level).
    5. "Making Sense with Outlines"—teaches outlining (intermediate level).
    6. "We Discover the Dictionary"—intermediate level
    7. "Who Makes Words?"—word origins (intermediate level)
    8. "Maps are Fun"—how to make and read maps (intermediate level)
    9. "How to Read a Book"—junior high
    10. "How to Remember"—junior high

11. "How to Study"—junior high
12. "Importance of Making Notes"—junior high
13. "Improve your Study Habits"—junior high
14. "Building an Outline"
15. "Reading Improvement: Comprehension Skills"
16. "Reading Imrpovement: Effective Speeds"
17. "Reading Improvement: Word-Recognition Skills"

30. *Craig Reader Programming*, Craig Corporation.

This offers individual reading improvement programs for elementary, junior and senior high, university, and adult education. All twelve programs are fully integrated for flexible application in developmental remedial and advanced levels; permit each student to gain maximum improvement through progress at his own individual rate.

31. *Phonetic Keys to Reading*, Economy Company.

This is a basal series for grades 1 through 3 emphasizing phonics from the beginning. The series consists of *Tag*, the preprimer; *Dot and Jim*, the primer; *All Around*, the first reader; *Through Happy Hours* and *As Days Go By* the second-grade readers; and *Along New Ways* and *Wide Doors Open*, the third-grade readers. The series is accompanied by teacher manuals, phonetic cards and charts, and picture cards. The intermediate program is termed *Keys to Independence in Reading*.

32. *Keys to Independence in Reading*, The Economy Company.

Keys to Independence in Reading continues the development of word-perception skills begun in Phonetic Keys to Reading, which are essential to success in all reading. Word perception is viewed not as a separate entity, but as being interrelated with the other basic aspects of comprehension and interpretation.

33. *EDL Filmstrips*, Educational Developmental Laboratories.

Filmstrips are available from readiness to adult levels. Readiness films are designed to develop concentration, observation, retention, discrimination, and logical reasoning while teaching sixty words. In grade 1 the pupil reads stories and adds 218 new words.

34. *Listen and Read Program*, Educational Developmental Laboratories.

This series of thirty tapes and workbooks helps the pupil to listen better, to understand words, sentences, and paragraphs, and introduces him to intensive, study-type reading, to critical reading, and to listening. The materials are on a junior-high–high-school level.

35. *Word Clues*, Educational Developmental Laboratories.

This series, for grades 7–13, teaches word knowledge by requiring the learner to divide the word into syllables, to pronounce it, to read it in a sentence, and to write a definition. It is accompanied by tests, flash-x sets with filmstrips and discs, and tach-x sets with filmstrips.

36. *Visual-Linguistic Basic Reading Series*, Education Press; Visual Products Division, 3M Company.

This program combines the visual, linguistic, listening, contextual, and programmed approaches. It consists of *Alphy's Show and Tell*, which is an alphabet unit, the preprimers, *Alphy's Cat and Alphy's Word Kit*, two primers (*Canny Cat* and *Baby Big Ear*), one reader (*Bob's Wish Cap*), four programmed texts, and printed originals for making transparencies.

37. *A to Z Phonics Charts*, Educational Publishing Corporation.
   This is a set of twelve charts teaching the basic elements of phonics. A manual, *A Guide to Teaching Phonics*, is provided to accompany the use of the charts.

38. *A First Course in Phonic Reading*, Educators Publishers Service.
   This first course is written for children in grades 2 and 3. *A Second Course in Phonic Reading I and II* (grades 4–5) is also available. These books are primarily intended for remedial reading.

39. *A First Course in Remedial Reading*, Educators Publishing Service.
   This book for second and third graders emphasizes phonic and kinesthetic approaches. In preparation are *A Second Course in Remedial Reading* (fourth and fifth grades) and *A Third Course in Remedial Reading* (junior high school).

40. *A Phonetic Reader Series*, Educators Publishing Service.
   These six books use phonetic methods. Although designed for the elementary grades, these readers could be valuable in a remedial junior-high situation. Titles included are *Puss in Boots; Jack, the Giant Killer; Jack and the Beanstalk; Aladdin and the Wonderful Lamp; Ali Baba and the Forty Thieves*, and *Robinson Crusoe*.

41. *First Phonics*, Educators Publishing Service.
   This program of two manuals, with *Stories for First Phonics*, and Drill Cards, is intended for first-grade children. It teaches phonics through the use of pictures.

42. *Remedial Training for Children with Specific Disability in Reading, Spelling, and Penmanship*, Educators Publishing Service.
   This manual comes with phonetic drill cards, phonetic word cards, *Syllable Concept, Little Stories, Introduction of Diphthongs*, and *Dictionary Technique*.

43. *Improving Word Skills*, Educators Publishing Service.
   This is a pupil workbook with an accompanying teacher's manual. It is designed for the intermediate grades and covers phonics, syllabication, and word parts.

44. *Learning the Letters*, Educators Publishing Service.
   This series of six booklets teaches the letters of the alphabet, their sounds, and common blends. It is intended primarily for remedial use.

45. *Programmed Phonics*, Educators Publishing Service.
   These two books, for grades 4–6, are designed for remedial teaching of phonics. There are three general objectives: (1) to train the student to attribute the proper sound to each letter in a word or syllable, (2) to train the student to perceive aurally and visually, and to respond vocally to each letter in a syllable and each syllable in a word in a left-to-right sequential order, and (3) to train the student to read whole words accurately and quickly. Assuming a fair understanding of initial and final consonant sound, Books 1 and 2 teach a basic phonic repertory, including a review of difficult consonants and of all

consonant blends. In addition, the student is trained to use principles of structural analysis and basic rules of pronunciation.

An aural-visual approach is used involving a workbook and either a tape or a script which may be read by the teacher. Each lesson presents several phonic elements through a series of auditory discriminations and dictations. The tape or script gives directions, prompts examples, and works through each frame and each page with the student. Having written a response, the student is informed immediately of the correctness or incorrectness of his answer. Correct answers are uncovered by moving a plastic mask down the page as the lesson progresses.

46. *Word Attack Manual*, Educators Publishing Service.

This manual is designed to strengthen word recognition and word meaning skill. It is to be used with junior high school youngsters. It covers closed and open syllables, long and short vowels, silent *e;* rules of syllable division; consonant letters and blends; digraphs; diphthongs; vowel *r* combinations; compound words, prefixes, and suffixes; accent; using the dictionary; *sh* sound of *ci, si,* and *ti;* the *y* sound of *i;* and the long *e* sound of *i.*

47. *Sounds for Young Readers*, Educational Record Sales.

This series from kindergarten to grade 5 (six records in all) is designed to help children with specific phonetic and auditory discriminatory difficulties.

48. *Sound Skills for Upper Grades*, Educational Record Sales.

These six records, for grades 5–9, provide help in consonant and vowel recognition and in word analysis.

49. *Visual Perception Skills*, Educational Record Sales.

These seven color filmstrips deal with visual memory, visual motor coordination, visual constancy, visual discrimination, visualization, figure-ground relationships, and visual matching.

50. *My Word Study Book*, Educational Service, Inc.

This series of six books, one for each grade, emphasizes phonetic sounds, syllabication, likenesses and differences, prefixes, and suffixes.

51. *Steps to Mastery of Words*, Educational Services, Inc.

These workbooks are designed for grades 1–6 and are accompanied by eight records.

52. *Alphy's Show and Tell Kits*, Education Services Press.

The first book teaches the names of the letters of the alphabet, their shapes, the alphabetical sequence, left-to-right projection, writing of the letters, and initial sound.

53. *American Phonetic Reader*, Expression Company.

This first reader, in which the lessons are graded, introduces phonetic symbols gradually.

54. *Fundamentals of Reading*, Eye Gate House.

These nine filmstrips are suitable for remedial junior high use and provide drill in mechanics of reading, phonetics, and reading comprehension.

55. *Phonics Handbook for the Primary Grades*, Feardon Publishers.
   This handbook contains many time-tested exercises and games.
56. *Come and Hear, A First Ear-Training Book*, Follet Publishing Co.
57. *Building Pre-Reading Skills: Kit A and Kit B*, Ginn and Company.
   Kit A contains 16 large illustrations, 60 smaller illustrations, and 112 still smaller illustrations. It is designed to help children develop the language, thinking, and perception skills necessary to success in learning to read.
   Kit B includes picture cards, word cards, letter cards, and a teacher's manual. The major purposes of Kit B are the following:
   1. To develop awareness of likenesses and differences in the initial sounds of spoken words.
   2. To develop auditory perception of the sounds represented by fifteen consonants in the beginning position (b, c, d, f, g, h, j, l, m, n, p, r, s, t, w).
   3. To teach association of the fifteen consonant sounds with the names and forms of the letters which represent them (phoneme-grapheme relationship).
   4. To teach use of context plus initial sounds to determine an oral response.
   5. To teach the lowercase and capital-letter forms of fifteen consonants.
58. *Sounds We Use*, Ginn and Company.
   These are twelve filmstrips, eight on consonants and four on vowels.
59. *Speech-to-Print Phonics*, Harcourt, Brace and World.
   This kit is a reading-readiness program. It contains flash cards, phonic lessons, and alphabet and consonant blend pads. Each lesson outlines an inductive introduction to each sound, words in which the sound is used, oral exercises with key words, and practice with flash cards and pupil pads.
60. *Word Attack: A Way to Better Reading*, Harcourt, Brace and World.
   This textbook is intended for remedial reading in high school. It uses contextual, auditory, structural, visual, and kinesthetic approaches. The exercises give training in the association of the printed symbol with the sound, utilization of word clues, analysis of prefixes, suffixes, and word roots, and development of dictionary skills.
61. *Reading Skills*, Holt, Rinehart and Winston, Inc.
   This text, with accompanying text booklet and shutter cards, is directed toward poorer readers at the junior-high level. The text includes training the eye to move correctly along the line, correcting lip movement, and subvocal meaning.
62. *Honor Products Programmed Materials*, Honor Products, Inc.
   These materials consist of a pushbutton testing machine and the following programs:
   1. *A Guide to Efficient Study* (grade 9)
   2. *Building Words* (grade 7).
   3. *Fun with Words-Homonyms* (grade 2)
   4. *Persuasive Words—Effective Word Usage* (grade 8)

5. *Reading Comprehension* (grade 9)
6. *Synonyms and Antonyms* (grade 9)
7. *Vocabulary Building* (grade 9)
8. *Word Clues* (grade 7)

63. *Language Master*, Hoover Brothers.
   For use with the language master machine are programs usable on all grade levels: The Vocabulary Builder Program, the Word-Picture Program, the Language-Stimulation Program, the Sounds of English Program, and the Phonics Program.

64. *A Practice Workbook on Phonetic Instruction*, Hough Community Project.
   This workbook is designed for junior-high use.

65. *Listen and Do*, Houghton Mifflin Company.
   Sixteen records, duplication masters for pupil worksheets, and a teacher's guide comprise the kit. It teaches the use of the context and initial sound in recognizing new words.

66. *Imperial Instructional Tapes*, Imperial Productions, Inc.
   The Imperial Primary reading program for grades 1–3 is a self-teaching program emphasizing readiness, study skills, comprehension skills, and word-attack skills. The program consists of forty tapes. Available from the same company is "The Easy Way to Difficult Sounds" program. This is a remedial phonic program on tape and chart. Available also is "The Alphabet and Its Sounds with Amos and his Friends."

67. *Early to Read Series*, Initial Teaching Alphabet Publications.
   This series by Mazurkiewicz and Tanyzer develops a phonetic alphabet of forty-four lowercase characters which represent the phonemes of the language. All the books and workbooks are designed for grade 1. The book titles are *Rides, Dinosaur Ben, Houses, A Game of Ball, The Yo-Yo Contest, Find a Way, The Tricks, The Bear that Moped*, and *Mr. Pickle's Surprise*. Available also are an alphabet book, sound symbol cards, vocabulary cards, and a word-building book.

68. *The Forty Sounds of English*, Initial Teaching Alphabet Publications.
   This film teaches the use of the initial teaching alphabet approach to reading instruction.

69. *Accelerated Progressive Choice Program*, Institute of Educational Research, Inc.
   This program proceeds from phonetically consistent letters to phonetically consistent compounds or letter groups to varying sounds for the same letter and varying letters for the same sound.

70. *I Learn to Read*, Kenworthy Educational Service.
   These two workbooks for grades 1–4 give a simplified course in phonics.

71. *Words in Color*, Learning Materials, Inc.
   This program contains *Words in Color: Background and Principles*, 21 colored charts, Phonic Code (8 charts in color), Word Cards. Books 1, 2, 3, *Word Building Book, Book of Stories*, and Worksheets.

72. *Tachist-o-Films*, Learning Through Seeing, Inc.
   These filmstrips on four levels, primary (grades 1–3), elementary (grades

4–6), junior high (grades 7–9), and senior high (grades 10–12), develop attention and concentration, build vocabulary, develop phrase-reading and uni-
tary-seeing, and improve retention, comprehension, and reading rate. Special
filmstrips cover phonics, prefix and suffix mastery, and word and phrase
mastery. A Tachist-o-Viewer is available.

73. *Tachist-o-Films and Tachist-o-Flasher*, Learning Through Seeing, Inc.,
   This is a phonics program for grades 1, 2, and 3. It teaches all the major
   phonic rules and concepts on a double-frequency approach—the most used
   sounds with the most frequently used words as examples.

74. *Basic Reading Series*, J. B. Lippincott.
   This is a program for grades 1–8, emphasizing a highly phonetic approach,
   and is accompanied by workbook and filmstrip materials.

75. *Readiness for Learning: A Program for Visual and Auditory Perceptual-Motor Training*, J. B. Lippincott.
   This program provides visual and auditory perceptual-motor training for
   kindergarten through grade 1. It involves bilateral and unilateral training and
   letter and word knowledge.

76. *Readiness for Learning Workbook*, J. B. Lippincott.
   The *Readiness for Learning Workbook* provides a carefully structured sequence of
   perceptual-motor training for kindergarteners or children beginning grade 1.
   It is divided into three levels of training. The first level deals with large-muscle,
   bilateral activities, aimed at developing coordination, control, comprehension
   of simple instructions, and conscious awareness of kinesthetic stimuli.
   The second level is concerned with the development of unilateral controls for
   the estblishment of eye-, hand-, and foot-dominance. The top level introduces
   some of the more specific skills needed in reading, such as knowledge of letter
   formations, perception of letter groupings, and the association of printed
   symbols with the spoken sounds and words they represent.

77. *Reading with Phonics*, J. B. Lippincott Company.
   This contains phonics books and three workbooks for grades 1-3.

78. *Phonics We Use*, Lyons and Carnahan.
   This is a phonics program for grades 1–8.

79. *Breaking the Sound Barrier*, Macmillan.

80. Deighton, Lee C.: Sanford, Adrian B., *et al.*, *The Macmillan Reading Spectrum*,
   Macmillan Company.
   This is a nongraded, multilevel program for building the vital reading skills.
   It consists of six word-analysis booklets, six vocabulary-development booklets,
   and six reading-comprehension booklets. Placement tests are provided. The
   lessons in the skill booklets are self-directing and self-correcting. Included
   also are two sets of books (60 in all) ranging from a second-grade reading
   level to eighth grade.

81. *Building Reading Skills*, McCormick Mathers Publishing Company, Inc.
   This phonic series contains workbooks with phonics exercises for grades 1–6.
   Included is a box of Teacher's Phonics Skill Builders—87 cards—and a
   guidebook.

82. *Conquests in Reading*, Webster Division, McGraw-Hill Book Company.
    This workbook for grades 4–6, is designed to review structural and phonetic skills by dealing with the basic relationships between consonant sounds and symbols, short-vowel sounds, sound blending, Dolch's Sight Words, silent letters, compound words, syllabication, prefixes and suffixes.

83. *Sullivan Programmed Reading*, Webster Division, McGraw-Hill Book Company.
    This is a fully-developed phonic reading program consisting of a prereading series and series I, II, and III. In all, twenty-one programmed workbooks are available.

84. *Time for Phonics*, Webster Division, McGraw-Hill Book Company.
    This is a phonics program for kindergarten through grade three. Book R is on the readiness level; Book A helps the pupil to recognize consonant sounds, the five short-vowel sounds, and the six consonant digraphs; Book B introduces the consonant blends, the long vowels, the vowel digraphs, phonic families, *y* as a vowel, long and short *oo*, and the diphthongs *ow-ou*, and *oy-oi*. Book C completes the phonics program.

85. *Eye and Ear Fun*, Webster Division, McGraw-Hill Book Company.

86. *Phonics is Fun*, Modern Curriculum Press.
    These six books for grades 1–3 are accompanied by three phonics workbooks.

87. *Phonics Workbooks*, Modern Curriculum Press.
    This set of three workbooks for grades 1–3 accompanies *Phonics is Fun* books for each grade level. The *Phonics is Fun* program consists of six books for grades 1–3.

88. *Audio-Visual Charts*, O'Connor Reading Clinic Publishing Company.
    Designed for primary and upper-elementary grades, these charts teach homophonous and homogeneous words. Cards emphasize such aspects as the *f* sound of *ph*, three sounds for *d*, the sound of *gh*, and the *z* sound of *s*.

89. *Instructor Basic Phonics Series*, F. A. Owen Publishing Company.
    This series contains five sets of materials: (1) Initial Consonant Sounds for grade 1; (2) Vowel Sounds for grades 1 and 2; (3) Advanced Consonants (blends) and Prepositions for grades 2 and 3; (4) Compounds, Suffixes, Prefixes, and Syllables for grades 2 and 3; and (5) Contractions and Advanced Phonic Forms for grades 3–5.

90. *The Reading Series*, Pacific Productions.
    This series of forty-one color filmstrips covers such areas as learning the use of the dictionary, phonetic analysis—vowels, structural analysis, reading for understanding, and using books efficiently.

91. *Phonovisual Skill Builders*, Phonovisual Products Inc.
    Accompanying the Consonant Chart and Method Book are the Readiness Book, the Transition Book, the Game Book, the Consonant Workbook, the Vowel Workbook, the Record of Sounds, the Consonant Flipstrips, the Magnetic Boards, Phonic Rummy Games, Consonant Picture Pack, and the Vowel Picture-Pack.

92. *New Auditory Visual Response Phonics*, Polyphone Company.
    This phonics program is a series of six teaching tapes, textbook, and worksheets to accompany the tapes and, if desired, the Polyphone, a ten- or fifteen-

outlet listening center. Letter sounds, blends, and various combinations are presented by tape and responded to on the worksheets with the aid of related pictures.

93. *Read Along with Me*, Programmed Records Inc.
This twelve-inch LP record and accompanying booklet are designed for the home instruction of beginning readers. The child follows the booklet as the words are spoken on the record.

94. *Lift-Off to Reading*, Science Research Associates.
This program for grades 1–6 is designed to provide a basal program to pupils who have poor motor, visual, verbal, or perceptual skills or who are mentally retarded or emotionally disturbed. It teaches reading for meaning, and controls the sequence of letter presentations and letter sound—letter shape relations.

95. *Reading in High Gear*, Science Research Associates.
This series of workbooks takes the culturally disadvantaged child and nonreader through a basic reading program. It is designed for grades 7–12 and adult level.

96. *S.R.A. Basic Reading Series*, Science Research Associates.
The Basic Reading Series for grades 1 and 2 is an inductive approach to beginning reading. It combines the best elements of phonics and whole-word reading-instruction methods. It focuses on decoding and introduces the child to 2300 words.

97. *Reading Laboratory Series*, Science Research Associates.
This series for grades 1–3 is the phonics portion of the Reading Laboratory Program. Although it is designed to supplement Laboratories 1a, 1b, and 1c in grades 1, 2, and 3, it may be used successfully in grades 4, 5, and 6. A teacher's handbook includes phonics lessons.

98. *Words and Patterns: A Spelling Series*, Science Research Associates.
For grades 2 and 3 this linguistically based program teaches spelling systematically, according to patterns of our language.

99. *Filmstrips for Practice in Phonetic Skills*, Scott, Foresman & Co.
There are four filmstrips for grade 1.

100. *Rolling Phonics*, Scott, Foresman & Company.
This is a set of blocks to be used in teaching phonics, both consonants and vowels. Teacher guides are available. The set is a part of the Linguistic Block Series, which includes *First Rolling Reader*, *Second Rolling Reader*, and *Third Rolling Reader*.

101. *Structural Reading Series*, F. W. Singer and Company.
This series begins with the spoken word as the basis of sound analysis. A readiness book, two first-grade readers, two second-grade readers, and phrase cards are available.

102. *Basic Primary Filmstrips Series*, Society for Visual Education.
This series for grades 1–3 includes:
  1. Initial Consonant Sounds—*b, d, p* (19 frames)
  2. Initial Consonant Sounds—*h, l, f, k* (23 frames)

   3. Initial Consonant Sounds—*m, n, t, j* (24 frames)
   4. Initial Consonant Sounds—*r, s, v, w* (25 frames)
   5. Initial Consonant Sounds—*c, g, y, q* (30 frames)
   6. *L* and *W* Blends—*bl, cl, fl, gl, pl, sl, sw, tw* (30 frames)
   7. *R* Blends—*br, cr, dr, fr, gr, pr, tr* (25 frames)
   8. *S* Blends—*sc, sk, sm, sn, sp, st* (25 frames)
   9. Two-letter Sounds—*ch, sh, wh, ph, th* (25 frames)
  10. Two and three-letter combinations—*kn, gn, wr, nd, ng, ck, nk, nt, gh, sch, squ, spl, spr, scr, str, thr* (29 frames)
  11. Rhyming Words and Final Consonant Sounds (31 frames)
  12. Short-Vowel Sounds (24 frames)
  13. Long-Vowel Sounds (25 frames)
  14. *Y*-Vowel Sounds (26 frames)
  15. Two-Letter Vowels (25 frames)
  16. Two-Letter Combinations—*oo, ow, ou, oi, oy, aw, au* (29 frames)
  17. Vowels controlled by *R* (28 frames)

103. *Basic Reading Series*, Society for Visual Education.
This basic reading series, in textfilm form to accompany the Lippincott Reading Series, consists of fifty-one filmstrips. This is a program for nursery schools, kindergartens, Head Start programs, early part of first grades, programs for slow learners, and non-English speaking children. The program consists of ten "See and Say" story picture books, five "See and Say" story records, two "Do and Learn" records, fourteen "Learning Activities," fourteen "Learning Charts," twenty-eight "Learning Chart Pads," forty-six "Animated Slides," and the teacher's planbook and handbook.

104. *Phono-Word Wheel sets*, Steck-Vaughn Company.

105. *Reading A*, Systems for Education, Inc.
Reading A, by Doman and Delacato, emphasizes the development of the child's perceptual ability. It consists of 330 Giant Word Cards, one Giant Teaching Book, a color picture book entitled *My Magic Words*, Make It Books, a Teacher's Manual, and a 32-frame four-color slide film of *My Magic Words* with sound recording pronouncing the words.

106. *Word Attack Series*, Teachers College Press.
This series of workbooks for grades 2–4 offers children a wide variety of approaches to reading new words.

107. *Eye and Ear Fun*, Webster Publishing Company.
This is a phonics program for grades 1–6. A separate book is provided for each of the first three grades; a fourth covers grades 4–6.

108. *It's Time for Phonics*, Webster Publishing Company.
These four workbooks for grade K–3 teach phonics in listening, speaking, reading, and writing.

109. *Webster Word Wheels*, Webster Publishing Company.
This is a set of sixty-three wheels that help individualize instruction in various phonics areas.

110. *Reading Seatwork Series*, Webster Publishing Company.

This series of workbooks for preprimer, primer, grade 1, and grade 2 is designed to develop word-recognition skills.

111. *Webster Word Wheels, Revised*, Webster Publishing Company.

These sixty-three wheels help teach consonant blends, prefixes, suffixes, and word blending. There are seventeen beginning blend wheels, twenty prefix wheels, eighteen suffix wheels, and eight 2-letter consonant wheels.

112. *Word Analysis Charts*, Webster Publishing Company.

These five charts are entitled Sounds the Letters Make, One-Syllable Words, Letters that Work Together, Prefixes Help Unlock Big Words, and Reading Big Words. They deal with consonant sounds, vowels, speech blends, vowel digraphs, prefixes, and syllabication.

113. *Writing Road to Reading*, Whiteside, Inc.

This book explains the Unified Phonics Method, using seventy phonogram cards. Cards may be reproduced or bought separately.

114. *Self Help Workbooks*, Whitman Publishing Company.

For ages 5–8, *Beginning Steps in Phonics* and for ages 6–9, *Next Steps in Phonics* are available.

115. *Sounds We Use*, Wilcox and Follett.

These three books are designed for grades 1–3.

116. *Syllabascope Materials*, Wordcrafters Guild.

This set of materials consists of *Teacher and Student Syllabascopes; Christie Word Set.* This contains sixty words of highest frequency in six intermediate readers series; *220 Basic Sight Words; Student Word Set; Guideword Dictionary*, and *Syllabication Principles.*

The materials are useful in teaching vocabulary, spelling, principles of word analysis, and syllabication. Using sliding panels, the pupil isolates the blends, affixes, and syllables from the total word so that he can study them individually and thus arrive at the total word.

Appendices

I

MULTIPLE SPELLINGS OF CONSONANTS

Ch: The *ch* sound may be spelled as *ch* (church) or as *tu* (nature, actual, future).

D: The *d* sound in verbs frequently is spelled *ed* (begged, bragged, canned and crammed). Usually the sound is spelled simply by *d* (as in *bed, fed, red*).

F: The *f* sound may be spelled as *f*, *ph*, or *gh*. In the words *fad, fan, fat, fed,* and *for,* the *f* is spelled as *f*. In *cough, draught, laugh, rough, tough, trough,* and *enough* the *f* is spelled as *gh*. In *phase, phew, phlegm, phone,* and *phrase* the *f* is spelled as *ph*. The *ph* spelling is common in scientific and medical terms of Greek origin (morphine, lymphatic, diaphragm, and diphtheria).

J: The *j* sound is spelled as *g* (magic), *ge* (page), *dg* (judgment), *dge* (judge), *ch* (Greenwich), and *di* (soldier). The most common spellings are *j*, *g*, *ge*, and *dge*. The *j* sound is spelled as *j* in *jam, jet, Jim, job;* it is spelled as *g* in *gem, gene, germ, gist;* it is spelled as *ge* in *age, barge, gauge, hinge;* and it is spelled as *dge* in *badge, bridge, budge, dodge.* The common spellings for *j* at the end of words are *ge* and *dge*.

K: The *k* sound is spelled as *c* (call), *cc* (account), *ch* (chorus), *ck* (back), *cu* (biscuit), *k* (rank), *qu* (liquor), and *que* (clique). The *c* spelling of *k* is most common (cat, can, come, came). Before *e* and *i* the initial *k* sound usually is spelled with a *k*. (keg, kept, kick, kid, kill, kin, king). *K* is also used in *khaki* and *kanaroo*.

A final *k* sound preceded by a consonant is usually spelled as *k* (ark, ask, balk, bark, bask). When the final *k* sound is preceded by a short-vowel sound as in *back, beck, black, buck,* and *click,* it is spelled as *ck*. A final *k* sound preceded by a long vowel has two options—*eke* or *eak, oak* or *oke.* In a medial position when the *k* sound begins a new syllable it is usually spelled *c*. There are many exceptions (yokel, market, basket, trinket, blanket, tinkle, twinkle, wrinkle, lamkin, manikin).

The student should become familiar with the various combinations of *act, ect, ict, oct, uct,* and *inct,* as in the words *fact, compact, elect, reject, depict, evict, concoct, conduct, instruct,* and *instinct.*

In words ending in *et* and *le* (ticket, jacket, pocket, rocket, bucket, tackle, sickle, trickle), the first syllable usually ends in *ck.* The *k* sound is spelled as *ch* in many Greek words (chasm, choir, Christ, chrism, chrome, scheme). It appears also, for example, in *ache, archive, chaos, chorus, school, character, chronology, echo, epoch, lichen, orchid, drachma,* and *troche.*

Finally, the *k* sound may be spelled as *que* (clique, unique, antique, mosque).

Ks: The *ks* sound is spelled as *ks, cks, cs, ks,* and *x.* Nouns ending in *k* form their plural by adding an *s;* the third person singular of verbs also ends in *s.* Usually, the *ks* sound at the end of words is an *x* (fix, mix, six). The *ks* sound may be spelled as *cc* before *e* or *i* (access, success).

S: The *s* sound may be spelled as *c, s,* or *sc.* Generally, the *c* or *sc* spelling occurs before *e, i, y.* The most common exceptions to this are *self, silk, system, sell, sent, site.* The final *s* sound may be spelled as *s, se,* or *ce.* Although most words end in *ence* or *ance,* some (dense, sense, expense, dispense, condense, intense, nonsense, defense, pretense, immense, recompense) end in *ense.*

Sh: The *sh* sound may be spelled as *sh* (ship), *ch* (machine), *sch* (schist), *ce* (ocean), *s* or *ss* (issue), *ti* or *si* (mission), *sci* (conscience); and *ci* (special). The *ch* spelling occurs commonly in words of French origin (cache, chef, gauche, chute, chandelier, Chicago, champagne, mustache, parachute, chiffon, stanchion, luncheon). The *sh* sound of *ci* is evident in *ferocious, ancient, glacial, spacious.* The *sh* sound of *s* or *ss* occurs in *fissure, issue, pressure, sure, sugar,* and *tissue.*

The pupil needs to learn the *sh* sound of *ti* and *si.* Numerous words in English are examples of this (compulsion, expulsion, impulsion, propulsion, immersion, submersion, aversion, diversion, ascension, comprehension, controversial, transient, vexatious, contentious, negotiate, partial, venetian, spatial, condition, expedition, ignition, ingratiate).

T: The *t* sound is spelled commonly as *t:* in past participles such as *clapped, dipped,* and *dripped,* it often is spelled *ed.*

Z: The *z* sound is spelled as *s, z,* and *x.* The pupil needs to become especially familiar with the suffixes *ize, lyze, ism*. Some common words in which the *z* sound is spelled as *s* are *is, his, was, has, rise, pose, wise, those, poise, these, tease, close, chose, prose, noise, cause, ease, lose, easel, use, cheese, abuse, amuse, propose, please, praise, confuse, dispose, infuse, busy, advise, advertise, exercise, surprise, blouse, accuse, rose, nose,* and *hose.*

Zh: The *zh* sound often is spelled as *s* or *z* (treasure, pleasure, collision, casual, azure, seizure).

II

THE SPEECH MECHANISM

Speech consists of the sound waves that are emitted by the human vocal mechanism. These sound waves strike the ear of another and elicit meaning from the recipient. Speech is a circular process. It is completed only when the sound waves (stimulus) elicit a response in a listener, that is, when they stir up meanings in another.

In most communication, and hence language, there is the intention to communicate something, the intention is then translated or encoded into symbols or words, and the necessary sounds are emitted. This latter process is termed *phonation*. The receiver of the communication in turn must hear the sounds (audition), must translate them (decoding), and must comprehend them.

Here we are not particularly concerned with how the speaker converts his idea, thought, or concept into sound waves nor how the recipient interprets them. We are interested in understanding the physiological process of speech.

To produce speech, the lungs, windpipe, glottis (Adam's apple), mouth, teeth, lips, and even the nose may be used. The lungs set the air into motion. The glottis contains the vocal cords. And the mouth contains the soft and hard palate and the tongue. The lips are used in producing *b, f, j, m, ch, p, sh, zh, v, w, wh;* the teeth are used in producing *f, s, v, th, z;* the tongue is used in producing *d, g, k, l, n, ng, r, t, y, ch, j, sh, th, zh;* the hard palate is used in producing *ch, d, l, j, n, t;* and the soft palate is used in producing *g, k, m, n, ng.*

The Vowels

Children quite early learn to articulate the short and long vowels. The production of the vowels begins with a muscular contraction of the lungs which forces a steady unobstructed air stream through the trachea, larynx, and pharynx to the outside. Vowels are thus called unobstructed sounds. Webster's Dictionary describes a vowel as "a speech sound in the articulation of which the oral part of the breath channel is not blocked and is not narrowed enough to cause audible friction." Sometimes the air passes through the oral cavities to the outside; sometimes it passes through the nasal cavities.

The larynx contains the vocal cords. In normal respiration the cords are widely separated at the back side. This produces unvoiced sounds. When the cords are almost closed, forcing the air through the narrow opening sets the cords into vibration and produces a voiced sound. Vowels are voiced sounds.

The size and shape of the mouth and the position of the lips and tongue determine what vowel will be produced. Three tongue parts (front, middle, and back), seven tongue heights, and two lip positions are identifiable. For example, the sounds *i* (bit), *e* (bet), *e* (the), *a* (bat), *a* (bar), *ea* (beat), *ai* (bait), *ay* (bay), *y* (by), *i* (bite), are produced by spreading or flattening the lips. The sounds *oo* (book), *a* (ball), *oo* (boot), and *oa* (boat), are produced by rounding the lips. The *oy* (boy) or *oi* (loin) sound begins with rounded lips, but ends with flattened lips. The *ou* (thou) sound is just the reverse. In Table IX we have listed the vowels of the English language and the possible spellings of each.

The Consonants

Consonants are produced by obstructing the air stream much as a structure in a hose obstructs the passage of water. Whenever the constriction in the breath channel is complete and is followed by a sudden release of the air as in *p*, *b*, *t*, *d*, *k*, and *g*, the consonant is called a plosive consonant. The soft palate is raised so the air does not pass through the nose.

Three of these consonants, *p*, *t*, *k*, are unvoiced sounds; *b*, *d*, and *g*, since their production requires the vibration of the vocal cords, are voiced sounds. When the production of the sound involves the use of the lips as in *p* and *b*, the sounds are labials. When sound production involves the use of the teeth or gum ridges, as in *t* and *d*, the sounds are dental. When the production of the sound involves the use of the soft palate, as in *k* and *g*, the sounds are called gutturals (velars).

D is produced by pressing the tip of the tongue against the upper teeth ridge and by blowing down the tongue while starting the voice at the same time. The production of *d* is thus áccompanied by a

TABLE IX

Common Vowel Sounds and Variant Spellings*

Symbol	Key Word	Variant Spellings
a	hat	plaid, ask, chaff.
ā	late	pain, day, break, veil, obey, gauge, eh, ay, chaotic, mellee.
ä	far	hearth, sergeant, memoir.
e(ə)	care	there, bear, chair, prayer, heir, e'er.
e	pet	heifer, leopard, friend, Aetna, feather, bury, any, said, says, Thames.
ē	be	feet, beam, deceive, people, key, Caesar, machine, police, field, quay, Phoebe, mete, create, fiasco.
(ə)r	ever	liar, elixir, actor, augur, pressure, glamour, zephyr.
i	bit	sieve, pretty, been, women, busy, build, hymnal, cottage, carriage, lyric, senate, mischief, circuit, forfeit, surface,
ə̇		mountain.
ī	ice	vie, rye, height, eye, aisle, aye, sky, buy, choir.
ä	not (short o sound)	was, hough.
ȯ	off	broth, cost, across, cough, loft.
	all	talk, haul, awe, Utah, Arkansas, law.
ȯ(ə) or ō(ə)	orb	orb, board, sword, court, borne, coarse, before, door, swarm, fought, memoir.
ō	old	oh, roam, foe, shoulder, grow, owe, sew, yeoman, beau, hautboy, brooch, soul, obey.
ə	sun (short u) sound)	come, nation, blood, double, does, twopence.
ə	canoe	banana, collect.
ə	fern	bird, urn, work, hurt, heard, journal, myrrh.
u̇	pull	wolf, Worcester, should, wood, foot, endure.
ü	use	unite, ewe, dew, beauty, feud, queue, lieu, cue, suit, yule.
	rude	brew, do, two, who, tomb, canoe, maneuver, blue, food, group, fruit, proof.
au̇	out	cow.
ȯi	soil	boil, oyster.

* Authorities disagree on the articulation of the vowels and consequently also on the number of different vowels. Vowel symbols used by permission. From Webster's Seventh New Collegiate Dictionary © 1969 by G. and C. Merriam Company, Springfield, Massachusetts, Publishers of the Merriam-Webster Dictionaries.

vocal-band vibration. The sound of *t* begins like *d*, but the blowing is so rapid that the breath escapes with an explosive result.

The *t* sound is an unvoiced dental plosive. It is made by obstructing the air stream and is followed by a sudden release of air. The soft palate is raised so the air does not pass through the nose. There is no vibration of the vocal cords in making the *t* sound, and it therefore is called an unvoiced sound. It is called a dental because in making the sound the tongue touches the upper gum ridge and then is quickly released, freeing a puff of air.

B is produced by closing the lips tightly and holding the teeth slightly apart. The lips are blown apart with a voiced breath. The *p* is made like the *b*, but there is no voicing.

G is produced with the lips and teeth slightly separated. The back of the tongue is raised against the back roof of the mouth. The tip of the tongue is kept behind the lower front teeth and the tongue is blown down suddenly with a voiced breath. *K* is made like *g* except that the slight explosion is voiceless.

The fricative or spirant consonants (*f*, *v*, *th*,* *s*, *z*, *sh*, *zh*, *j*, and *ch*) are formed by partially closing the air passage. These sounds can be prolonged indefinitely and usually are accompanied by friction. To produce the labiodental fricatives (the unvoiced *f* and the voiced *v*), the upper teeth are in contact with the lower lip. Breath is forced out as the teeth and lip touch. When the sound is voiced, it is a *v*; when it is unvoiced, it is an *f*.

The production of both the voiced and unvoiced dental fricative *th* requires contact between the tip of the tongue and the back of the upper front teeth. The teeth and lips are slightly apart.

To produce the unvoiced *s* the air stream is allowed to pass through a narrow opening between the tip of the tongue and the gums. The front teeth are closed and the entire tongue is raised and grooved along the midline. The tip of the tongue is placed about a quarter of an inch behind the upper teeth. The soft palate is raised. The *s* sounds like air going out of a tire. The voiced *z* requires a slightly larger opening and the teeth are separated.

The unvoiced *sh* as in *ship* is produced much like the *s*, but the air stream is forced over a broader surface than for the *s*. The tongue is raised and drawn back, the lips are rounded, and the soft palate is raised. The *zh* is the same sound as the *sh* except that it is voiced.

The unvoiced *ch* is produced by making the *t* sound and quickly exploding it into a *sh* sound. The tip of the tongue touches the upper gum ridge and then is quickly released, freeing a puff of air and

---

* *Th* as in *then* (voiced) and in *thin* (unvoiced). The unvoiced *th* occurs, for example, in *birth, booth, breath, broth, cloth, both, death, depth, doth, earth, faith, fourth, length, mouth, north,* and *path.* The voiced *th* occurs in *than, that, their, these, they, therefore, those, thus, bathe, breathe, clothe, scathe, smooth, sooth, with, although, brother, either, father, other,* and *gather.*

producing a *t* sound. This then is quickly changed to the *sh* sound. The *j* sound is voiced and made by raising the front part of the tongue toward the teeth ridge and hard palate. The sounds *ch* and *j* (which is produced like *ch*) sometimes are called plosives. More correctly, they are affricates in that they begin as plosives and end as fricatives.

The nasals or linguals (*m*, *n*, and *ng*) are formed by completely closing the mouth and allowing the air to escape through the nasal cavities. The soft palate is lowered and each sound is voiced. Closed lips prevent the air from passing through the mouth in the production of *m*. The teeth are slightly apart and a humming sound is sent through the nose. For *n* the tip of the tongue is pressed against the gums. The tongue is not dropped and the mouth is not closed until the sound has been made. For *ng* the tongue is raised against the soft palate. The tongue is kept in this position until a voiced sound is sent through the nose.

The semivowels or glides (*y*, *hw*, *w*, *l*,* *r** and *h*) are produced by a gliding movement of the tongue or lips from one place to another. They are produced when the vocal organs are getting ready to produce another sound. The passage from the vocal cords to the outside is partially blocked. The voiced *r* before a vowel, as in *rabbit* or *train*, is produced by raising the tip of the tongue toward the gum ridge without actual contact. The teeth are slightly separated and a curl is formed down the middle of the tongue.

The voiced *l* is produced by elevating the tip of the tongue toward the upper gum ridge. Contact is made, and the air passes over the sides of the tongue. The soft palate is raised for making both sounds. Some describe the *l* sound as the " peanut butter sound." As the sound is made, it feels as though one were wiping peanut butter from the roof of the mouth.

The *hw* is produced like a *w* without vibration of the vocal cord. It is an unvoiced fricative. To produce the voiced *w* the lips are rounded and an opening is left for the air to emerge from the mouth. The tip of the tongue is raised back of the lower teeth. In teaching the sound, the teacher might ask the child to blow out a lighted candle while saying *while* or *what*. The *w* is like a vowel in that it is pro-nounced in a vowel position and like a consonant in that it is pro-

---

* *L* and *r* at the end of a word, as in *water* and *panel*, are not glides.

TABLE X

THE CONSONANT SOUNDS OF THE LANGUAGE

Plosives		Fricatives		Nasals	Semivowels	
Voiced	*Unvoiced*	*Voiced*	*Unvoiced*	*Voiced*	*Voiced*	*Unvoiced*
b	p	th	th	m	r	h(hw)
d	t	v	f	n	l	
g	k	z(azure)	s	ng	y	
		zh(rouge)	sh		w	
		j	ch			

nounced with audible friction. *H* generally is an unvoiced sound; *y* is a voiced sound.

Like the *w*, the *y* has the position of a vowel but the friction of a consonant. The front tip of the tongue is raised nearly to the hard palate behind the upper teeth. The side of the tongue touches the side of the teeth, and the teeth and lips are slightly apart. *H* should be sounded with a vowel. When *h* occurs between vowels, it may be a voiced sound. The vowel determines the position of the tongue and lips. The air is blown outward and the tongue is behind the lower teeth. In Table X we have listed the various consonant sounds in the language.

III
MULTIPLE SPELLING OF VOWELS

T HE spelling of vowel sounds presents many more difficulties for the pupil. In the first place, there are so many alternatives. However, the teacher, if not the pupil, may benefit from knowing what these alternatives are. Table XI lists the most common spellings for the long and short vowel sounds.

TABLE XI

Multiple Spellings of Vowels

short a	long a	long u	ȯ
a (bat)	a (lake)	eau (beauty)	o (off)
ai (plaid)	ai (pain)	eu (feud)	ou (cough)
	au (gauge)	ew (few)	
short e	ay (day)	ewe (ewe)	ȯ or ȯ(ə)
a (any)	ea (break)	ieu (lieu)	o (orb)
ae (aetna)	ei (veil)	ou (you)	a (all)
ai (said)	ey (obey)	ueue (queue)	au (caught)
ay (says)	eigh (weight)	u (use)	aw (awe)
e (pet)	a-e (safe)	ue (cue)	ah (Utah)
ea (feather)		ui (suit)	as (Arkansas)
ei (heifer)	long e	u-e (mule)	oa (board)
eo (leopard)	ae (Caesar)		ou (court)
ie (friend)	ay (quay)		oi (memoir)
u (bury)	e (be)	ä	
	ea (beam)	a (far)	ou
short i	ee (feet)	ea (hearth)	ou (out)
e (pretty)	ei (deceive)	e (sergeant)	ow (cow)
ee (been)	eo (people)	oi (memoir)	
i (sit)	ey (key)		oi
ia (carriage)	i (machine)	e(ə)	oi (boil)
ie (sieve)	ie (field)	a (care)	oy (oyster)
o (women)	oe (phoebe)	e (there)	
u (busy)	e-e (these)	ea (bear)	ə
ui (build)		ai (chair)	u (urn)
y (hymnal)	long i	ay (prayer)	e (fern)
	ai (aisle)	ei (heir)	i (bird)
short o(ä)	ay (aye)	e'er (e'er)	o (work)
a (was)	ei (height)		ea (heard)
o (not)	ey (eye)	i(ə)	ou (journal)
ou (hough)	i (ice)	e (here)	y (myrrh)
	ie (vie)	ea (fear)	eu (jeu)
short u	igh (high)	ei (weird)	o (können)
io (nation)	oi (choir)	ee (deer)	u̇
o (come)	uy (buy)	ie (bier)	ooo
oe (does)	y (sky)	i (fakir)	oo (foot)
oo (blood)	ye (rye)		o (wolf)
ou (double)	i-e (pine)	ər	ou (should)
u (sun)	y-e (type)	e (ever)	u (pull)
wo (twopence)		a (liar)	ü
	long o	i (elixir)	oo
	au (hautboy)	o (actor)	oo (food)
	e (sew)	u (augur)	ew (brew)
	eau (beau)	ou (glamour)	o (ado)
	eo (yeoman)	y (zephyr)	wo (two)
	o (old)		oe (canoe)
	oa (roam)	ə	eu (maneuver)
	oe (foe)	a (senate)	ue (blue)
	oh (oh)	ai (mountain)	u (endure)
	oo (brooch)	ay (always)	ou (group)
	ou (shoulder)	ei (forfeit)	ui (fruit)
	ou (soul)	eo (pigeon)	u-e (rule)
	ow (grow)	e (women)	
	o-e (home)	ie (mischief)	

IV

TWO-SYLLABLE WORDS ILLUSTRATING PHONIC SKILLS

Two-Syllable Words Illustrating the Beginning and End Consonant Blends

abbess	clinic	endless	intact	restless	stopgap
abduct	clipping	enlist	intend	rostrum	stuffing
abrupt	closet	entrap	intent	sampling	suspect
absent	collect	figment	invent	sandbag	suspend
acting	command	filling	invest	scalpel	swelling
adapt	commend	flagstaff	itself	scallop	swimming
addict	comment	flannel	justness	scandal	swindling
address	compact	flatcar	killing	scanner	switchboard
adduct	compress	fretful	kindred	scanty	switchman
adept	conduct	fulcrum	kinsman	scapegoat	tactful
adopt	confess	fungus	lament	scarcely	talent
adrift	conflict	garland	lasting	scarecrow	tactless
adult	congress	gastric	lefthand	scatter	tantrum
advent	connect	gladness	leftist	sceptic	tempting
affect	consent	glisten	listless	scolding	tenant
alarm	consist	gravel	Madrid	scornful	torrent
amass	constant	handbag	misspell	Scotsman	torrid
amend	construct	handcuff	mustang	Scottish	traffic
anthill	contact	handful	neglect	scoundrel	transcribe
arctic	contend	harmful	nostril	scraper	transect
ardent	content	harmless	nostrum	sculpture	transgress
armful	contest	helpful	object	scurry	transmit
arming	contract	helping	obsess	scurvy	transplant
armpit	contrast	helpless	offend	schedule	Trappist
artful	convent	himself	oppress	schema	travel
artist	convict	hundred	parting	scholar	trellis
aspect	corrupt	hunting	patent	schooling	trespass
assent	dentist	husband	pedant	schooner	triplet
assess	disband	impart	pending	segment	tropic
asset	discard	implant	pilgrim	settling	trumpet
attend	direct	impress	placard	smallness	unarm
attest	disgust	imprint	plastic	solvent	unbend
attract	dispend	indent	plated	Spartan	unblest
babbling	disrupt	induct	platting	spastic	undress
badlands	dissent	indult	pregnant	spectrum	unharmed
baldness	distant	indwell	present	spelling	unjust
ballast	distinct	inept	pressing	spinning	unrest
bandstand	distract	infant	problem	spital	unsnap
banging	district	infect	product	spotless	upend
bangup	distrust	infest	profit	spotted	upheld
Baptist	draftsman	inflict	progress	stagnant	uplift
bobsled	dragnet	inject	prospect	standing	uphill
bonded	drama	inland	pumpkin	standstill	upstart
brisling	dressing	insect	rambling	static	upswing
bullfrog	enact	insist	rampant	stigma	wettest
clement	encamp	inspect	rattling	stillness	winded
cleric	emblem	instill	restful	stockyard	windmill
clevis	ending	insult	resting	stolid	windfall

164

Two-Syllable Words Illustrating the
k & *qu* Sounds

k	hassock	kinsman ____	potluck	spoken	weekday
	heckle	kitten	prickly	spunky	weekly
akin	homelike	kitty	provoke	stick-up	weeping
backstop	homesick	Kodak	racket	sticky	wicked
backup	inkstand	lanky	rankle	stinking	winking
balky	inkwell	lipstick	rebuke	stockpile	
baking	intake	locket	reckless	stuckup	*Q-Kw*
banking	invoke	lockup	remark	swanky	
bankrupt	jackal	lucky	restock	sunstruck	acquit
barrack	jackass	makeup	rickets	sunken	banquet
basket	jacket	market	risky	tackle	cònquer
beckon	jockey	markup	rocket	ticket	conquest
blacken	lampblack	monkey	rocky	ticking	frequent
blanket	keepsake	musket	silken	tinkle	inquest
bracket	kennel	muskrat	silky	token	inquire
bucket	Kenny	napkin	skeptic	trademark	liquid
casket	kettle	necktie	skillful	trinket	misquote
cockpit	keyboard	numskull	skillet	trickle	quicken
cracking	keyhole	o'clock	skimming	tricky	quinine
darken	keynote	packet	skimpy	twinkle	quintile
darkness	kidnap	pancake	skinny	unlike	quisling
embark	kidney	peacock	skylark	unlock	quorum
fullback	kindle	picket	skylight	unpack	request
frisky	kindling	picking	slapstick	waken	require
freckle	kindly	pickle	socket	weakness	sequel
frankly	kindness	planking	sneaky	weaken	tranquil
frankness	kindred	plucky	sparkle	weakling	
flapjack	kingly	pocket	speaking	wisecrack	
gasket	kinky	postmark	speckle	wedlock	

Two-Syllable Words Illustrating the Long-Vowel Sounds

Long a	fragrant	satrap	beyond	reject	bridal
	gable	slavish	demon	replant	client
able	gravy	staple	emit	reprint	climax
ably	hasten	stapler	equal	resell	crisis
baby	hasty	status	hero	reset	diet
bacon	hatred	stable	Jesus	resource	dinette
basal	ladle	scaly	legal	respell	diving
basic	lady	table	maybe	retail	filing
basin	naked	taking	meter	retake	finite
basis	nasal	tasteful	pean	retell	gliding
blatant	native	tasty	Peking	retest	grimy
cradle	navy	trader	predate	retrace	hiding
craving	papal	trading	prefect	secret	idol
data	patron	vagrant	react	Swedish	irate
datum	rapist	*Long e*	recall		ivy
David	rating		recap	*Long i*	libel
flaming	sacred	acne	refill		lilac
fracas	sadism	bebop	refund	bison	liking
flaky	Satan	being	regal	biting	lining

microbe	wiring	milepost	signpost	sputum	losing
migrant	wiry	moment	silo	stupid	move
migrate		mores	sixfold	student	movement
mining	*Long o*	Moses	slogan	tuba	movie
minus		mostly	sloping	tubing	prove
nitrate	afford	motel	smolder	tulip	remove
piling	ago	motif	sober	tumult	two
pilot	banjo	motive	sofa	tunic	twofold
primate	bingo	motto	soldier	unit	twosome
riding	broken	noble	sportsman		twostep
rifle	cargo	nobly	sporty	*u = ü*	undo
riot	clover	obese	stoic		who
ripen	cobra	okay	stolen	hurrah	whom
rival	coed	omit	story	include	whose
silent	deport	oral	stucco	intrude	womb
silo	enroll	oval	swollen	Judith	
sinus	florist	passport	tempo	judo	*Long y*
siren	focus	patrol	tollbooth	Judy	
stifle	global	poem	tonal	junior	apply
spinal	glory	poet	tonus	Pluto	comply
spiral	going	polite	topmost	prudence	defy
spirant	golden	polo	Tory	prudent	deny
stipend	grotto	pony	total	prudish	flying
tidy	hero	portal	totem	ruble	hydrant
tiger	holy	portrait	transport	rubric	hygiene
tigress	hostess	postal	Trojan	ruby	hyphen
tiling	hotel	postman	trophy	ruthless	imply
timing	import	probate	veto		nylon
tiny	impose	profess	woven	*o as ü*	pigsty
tiring	inmost	program			prying
Titan	jumbo	protest		approve	rely
tithing	Kodak	protract		do	reply
title	limbo	report	fuel	doing	spyglass
triad	lingo	repose	fury	doer	stylist
trial	local	robust	humid	hairdo	stylus
tribal	locus	rodent	mural	improve	supply
trident	locust	rolling	music	into	typing
trifle	lotto	rosy	puny	lose	typist
tripod	lotus	roving	pupil	loser	tyrant

Two-Syllable Words Having a Long Middle Vowel and Ending in a Silent *e*

a + e	behave	create	farewell	inmate	mistake
	blameless	debate	filtrate	innate	namely
aflame	blockade	declare	frustrate	insane	namesake
arcade	brigade	dictate	gamely	invade	narrate
awake	butane	donate	grapevine	irate	negate
aware	careful	engrave	grateful	keepsake	nitrate
bareback	careless	erase	homemade	landscape	octane
barely	classmate	escape	inane	lately	parade
baseball	compare	estate	inflame	locate	placate
basement	conclave	evade	inflate	mandate	plateful
became	crankcase	fanfare	inhale	migrate	plate-glass

predate	afire	ignite	umpire	homely	assume
probate	alike	imbibe	unite	homemade	astute
profane	alpine	incline	unlike	homesick	capsule
prostrate	arise	inside	unripe	hopeful	commune
regale	arrive	inspire	widely	hopeless	commute
relate	aside	invite	wideness	ignore	compute
resale	aspire	landslide	windpipe	implore	conclude
restate	backfire	lifeless	winesap	inclose	confuse
retake	barbwire	likely	wireless	invoke	consume
rotate	beside	liken		keyhole	costume
safety	besides	likeness	*o + e*	keynote	diffuse
salesman	bonfire	likewise		lonely	dilute
sameness	clockwise	limestone	abode	lonesome	dispute
statesman	collide	lineman	adore	manhole	disuse
stagnate	combine	lively	afore	microbe	endure
stalemate	compile	meantime	alone	milestone	immune
sulfate	comprise	milepost	arose	nosebleed	impure
sedate	confide	milestone	atone	noteless	impute
tapeline	conspire	nineteen	backbone	oppose	infuse
telltale	contrite	ninety	before	parole	legume
tradesman	contrive	offside	cajole	promote	mature
translate	decline	polite	commode	propose	minute
unsafe	define	profile	condone	remote	misuse
	demise	provide	console	restore	pollute
e + e	deprive	recline	demote	sandstone	prelude
	desire	refine	denote	stovepipe	procure
adhere	despise	repine	deplore	smokestack	purely
compete	divide	retire	depose	sunstroke	refuse
complete	divine	rewire	devote	seashore	refute
concrete	empire	senile	disclose	toneless	resume
convene	enquire	spineless	elope	transpose	secure
delete	entire	spiteful	enclose	trombone	tribune
gangrene	esquire	spitfire	erode		tribute
impede	finite	tapeline	evoke	*u + e*	unused
stampede	firearm	tideland	flagpole		useful
	firebug	timecard	gallstone	abuse	useless
i + e	fireman	timeless	galore	accuse	
	firefly	timely	hailstone	acute	*y + e*
abide	fireside	tireless	homeless	allude	
admire	grapevine	tiresome	homelike	allure	retype
advise	homelike	transpire			

Two-Syllable Words Having a Long First Vowel and a Silent Second Vowel

ai	airline	await	declaim	failing	mainland
	airmail	bailee	despair	failure	mainly
affair	airplane	bailiff	derail	faintly	painful
afraid	airport	barmaid	detail	fairly	painted
ailment	airraid	blackmail	detailed	fairness	pigtail
aircraft	airship	bridesmaid	detain	faithful	plaintiff
airdrome	airstrip	complain	disclaim	faithless	portrait
airfield	airtight	complaint	disdain	hailstone	proclaim
airlift	armchair	contain	entrails	inlaid	railing

				ie	*oe*
railroad	payee	measles	between		
railway	payment	meaty	breeding		
rainbow	playful	misdeal	canteen	allied	tiptoe
raincoat	playmate	mislead	careen	applied	toein
raindrop	playtime	mistreat	career	belie	toenail
rainfall	railway	nearest	carefree	implied	
rainy	relay	oatmeal	coffee	tie-up	*oo*
reclaim	repay	peaceful	decree	untie	
refrain	replay	peanut	degree	untried	backdoor
remain	saying	pleading	deepen		flooring
repaint	speedway	pleasing	esteem	*oa*	indoor
retail	spillway	reading	flywheel		
retain	subway	real	freely	aboard	*ow*
sailing	Sunday	repeal	freewill	abroad	
saintly	seaway	repeat	freedom	afloat	aglow
stainless	wayside	reread	gleeful	approach	arrow
sustain		retreat	greedy	bemoan	bellow
unpaid	*ea*	smeary	inbreed	billboard	bellows
waistband		stealing	indeed	boatman	below
waistline	beacon	steamboat	keeping	broadcast	bestow
waiting	beaming	spearmint	keepsake	carload	blowing
waitress	bearded	seaman	linseed	coating	borrow
	beastly	seamless	misdeed	cocoa	bowling
ay	beaten	seashore	needle	floating	disown
	beneath	seaway	needless	foamy	follow
array	cleanly	teacher	needy	housecoat	gallows
astray	cleanness	teacup	nineteen	iceboat	glowing
away	creamy	teammate	nosebleed	inroad	hollow
betray	daydream	teamster	payee	keyboard	lowland
daytime	dealing	teamwork	redeem	loading	lowly
daylight	decrease	teapot	seedling	oatmeal	mellow
defray	defeat	tearful	seemly	potroast	minnow
delay	disease	teaspoon	teeming	railroad	narrow
display	dreamland	treatment	teepee	raincoat	owing
essay	dreamy	unclean	teething	reload	pillow
folkway	dreary	unseat	treetop	reproach	rainbow
Friday	freaky	weakness	trustee	roaring	rowboat
gayness	greasy	weary	unseen	rowboat	sallow
highway	hearing	weasel	upkeep	soapsuds	snowball
layer	impeach		weedless	soapy	snowblind
layette	increase	*ee*	weeper	steamboat	snowfall
layoff	leading		weever	scapegoat	snowflake
maybe	leafless	agree	weevil	topcoat	snowy
mayor	leaflet	agreed		unload	sorrow
midday	leaky	asleep		uproar	sparrow
Monday	leasing	beefsteak			widow
okay	meantime	beehive			willow
					window

Two-Syllable Words Illustrating the
v, *x*, *y*, and *z* Sounds

v	valley	vestige	axis	extend	yeoman
	valor	vestment	axle	extent	yiddish
avail	value	veto	axon	extinct	yielding
avid	vampire	vibrant	beeswax	extol	yoked
bereave	vandal	vibrate	betwixt	extra	
carving	Vandyke	vicar	boxer	extract	*z*
devil	vanguard	victim	complex	extreme	
even	vanish	victor	convex	icebox	baptize
event	vanquish	viewless	exact (gz)	index	bazaar
evil	vantage	viewpoint	exalt (gz)	influx	bizarre
gavel	vapid	vigil	exam (gz)	matrix	breezy
giver	varment	vigor	exceed	maxim	crazy
govern	varnish	vintage	excel	mixer	dazzle
graveyard	vary	vinyl	except	oxcart	dizzy
gravy	vassal	virgin	excess	prefix	frenzy
harvest	vastness	virile	exchange	pyrex	enzyme
havoc	vaulted	virus	excise	reflex	fizzle
lavish	vector	viscose	excite	saxon	gazelle
leaving	veiling	visit	exclaim	toxic	gizzard
novel	vellum	vital	exclude	waxy	glazier
pelvic	velvet	vivid	excuse		glazing
pelvis	venal	vocal	exempt (gz)	*y*	grazing
prevail	vender	vodka	exhale		grizzly
prevent	vendor	voiceful	exhaust (gz)	barynard	guzzle
preview	veneer	volley	exhort (gz)	lawyer	hazy
revel	ventral	volume	exile	yachting	lazy
revere	Venus	vomit	exist (gz)	yammer	Ozark
revile	verbal	vortex	exit	yankee	plaza
revise	verdict	voucher	expand	yardage	pretzel
revoke	vermin	vouchsafe	expanse	yardman	puzzle
revolt	version	vowel	expect	yardstick	puzzling
rivet	versus	vulgar	expel	yearbook	zealous
vaccine	vertex	vulgate	expense	yearling	zebra
vagrant	very		expire	yearly	zero
valance	vesper	*x as ks*	explode	yeasty	zipper
valet	vessel		expose	yellow	zither
valid	vestal	affix	express		

Two-Syllable Words Illustrating the
ch, *sh*, *th*, *wk*, *gh*, and *ph* Sounds

ch	charcoal	cheery	chimney	chortle
	chattel	chemist (k)	chipmunk	chorus (k)
attach	cheapen	cherish	chirrup	chosen
backache (k)	cheapskate	cherry	chitchat	Christen (k)
beseech	checkbook	chicken	chloride (k)	Christian (k)
catcher	checkmate	childlike	chopping __	Christmas (k)
catching	cheerful	children	choppy	chronic (k)
chapel	cheerly	chilly	choral (k) __	chuckle

chummy	fishy	shellac	Martha	whereas
chunky	flashlight	shelter	plaything	whereat
cockroach	flashy	shelving	Sabbath	wherefore
detach	flagship	shepherd	thankful	wherein
discharge	finish	sherbet	thankless	whether
dispatch	gunshot	sheriff	theism	whimper
etching	hardship	sherry	theist	whipping
franchise	impish	shiftless	themselves	whirlpool
enrich	Irish	shifty	thereby	whisker
godchild	lavish	shilling	therefore	whiskey
headache (k)	marshal	shimmer	therein	whiten
itchy	marshy	shiner	thermal	whiteness
ketchup	midship	shingle	thesis	whitler
kitchen	parish	shining	thicken	whiting
machine (sh)	pettish	shiny	thicket	whitish
orchard	piggish	shipment	thievish	whittle
orchid (k)	polish	shipmate	thimble	
ostrich	refresh	shipshape	thinking	*ph*
parchment	relish	shipwreck	thirsty	
Rachel	reshape	shipyard	thirteen	asphalt
ranchman	rubbish	shirker	thirty	blaspheme
sandwich	selfish	shiver	thistle	digraph
satchel	shabby	shoddy	thither	gopher
technic (k)	shackle	shoeblack	thorax	graphic
technique (k)	shadow	shoehorn	thorny	hyphen
	shady	sluggish	thoughtful	nephew
sh	shakedown	snapshot	thoughtless	orphan
	shaking	Spanish	thrashing	phantom
afresh	shaky	windshield	threaten	pheasant
ashamed	shallow		threefold	phoneme
ashes	shamble	*th*	threescore	phoney
backlash	shameful		thresher	phonic
banish	shameless	athlete	threshold	phony
bashful	shampoo	bequeath	throttle	Phyllis
bishop	shamrock	betroth	throughout	physique
blemish	Shanghai	breathing	thunder	prophet
bushel	shanty	breathless	Thursday	rephrase
bushy	shapeless	clothing	thyself	siphon
camshaft	shapely	deathbed		sophist
clavish	sharpen	deathly	*wh*	triumph
codfish	sharper	dishcloth		trophy
dashboard	sharpness	ethic	awhile	
dishrag	shatter	ethnic	elsewhere	*gh*
freshman	shaving	filthy	meanwhile	
freshness	shebang	gather	whaler	aghast
English	sheepish	Gothic	whaling	ghastly
famish	sheepskin	lengthen	wheedle	ghostly
fishing	sheeting	lengthy		

The Soft Sounds of *c* and *g*

c					
	accent	advice	cement	cigar	civil
	accept	airforce	censure	citrus	commence
absence	access	allspice	census	city	conceal
accede	acid	cancel	central	civics	concede

conceit	iceboat	process	allege	enrage	infringe
conceive	icebox	produce	arrange	gadget	ingest
consent	icecream	province	avenge	gender	judge
decease	icehouse	recede	begrudge	genius	judgment
deceased	iceman	receive	besiege	gentle	language
deceit	iceplant	recept	budget	gentry	legend
deceive	icing	recess	cartridge	genus	legion
decent	icy	recite	challenge	gerund	luggage
decide	incite	replace	cogent	gesture	manager
decile	lacing	retrace	deluge	giant	misjudge
deduce	lucid	stencil	digit	giblet	pudgy
deice	mercy	tacit	digest	ginger	pungent
denounce	parcel	tracing	discharge	giraffe	ranger
device	precede		divulge	gypsy	rechange
fancy	precept	*g*	frigid	hygiene	refuge
embrace	princely		engage	immerge	regent
graceful	princess	aged	engaged	impinge	regime
iceberg	proceed	agent	enlarge	indulge	

Two-Syllable Words in Which *s* is Pronounced as *z*

abuse	chisel	enclose	menses	preside	rosy
accuse	clockwise	gallows	miser	propose	soapsuds
advise	closet	grisly	mores	quisling	sometimes
arise	demise	impose	monism	raisin	thousand
arose	depose	inclose	Moses	reason	Thursday
badlands	desert	infuse	nosebleed	refuse	tradesman
beeswax	deserve	ism	nudism	repose	transpose
bellows	desire	Jesus	oppose	resent	unused
baptism	desist	Joseph	pheasant	resist	visit
besides	despise	kinsfolk	physics	result	weasel
bridesmaid	disclose	leasing	pleasing	resume	wisecrack
cheesecloth	disease	likewise			

Two-Syllable Words Illustrating the Three-Letter Consonant Blends: *scr, shr, spl, spr, squ, str,* and *thr*

scr	*shr*	*spr*	*str*		*thr*
			stratum		
			streaky		
inscribe	shriner	sprayer	abstract	streamer	dethrone
prescribe	shrinkage	spreader	constraint	streetcar	thrasher
proscribe	shrivel	springtime	construct	strengthen	threaten
scrabble	shrubby	sprinkle	instruct	stretcher	threefold
scramble			obstruct	striate	threshold
scrappy	*spl*	*squ*	straddle	stringy	thrifty
scratcher			straighten	stroller	throaty
scratchy	splashy	squabble	strainer	strongly	throttle
scrawny	splendid	squadron	stranger	struggle	
scribble	splendor	squander	strangle	strutter	
scrimmage	splinter	squirrel	strata		
scripture					

Two-Syllable Words with Long Vowels in the Medial Position Between Two Consonants

long i	lightning	finding	*(int)*	unsold	costly
	limelight	hindsight		uphold	defrost
(igh)	mighty	kindless	pint-size		doggie
	nightly	kindly		*(oll)*	dogma
brighten	nightmare	kindness	—*(imb)*		frosty
bullfight	nighttime	mankind		tollgate	frosting
daylight	rightful	mindful	climber	unroll	frostbite
delight	rightly	mindless	climbing		glossy
flighty	rightness	remind		*The o sound of o*	kickoff
frighten	spotlight		*Long o*		lofty
gaslight	stoplight	*(ild)*		*(of-off-og-oth-*	often
highness	tightrope		*(old)*	*oss-ost-ong-off-*	prologue
highway	twilight	mildness		*oft-ough)*	toffee
hindsight		wildcat	behold		toss-up
insight	*(ind)*	wildfire	billfold	across	upmost
midnight		wildness	blindfold	aloft	utmost
lighting	behind	wildly	holding	along	watchdog
lightly	binding		tenfold	belong	wrongly
lightness	blindfold		unfold	coffin	

The Effect of r on Previous Vowel

ar = ər	medlar	warden	blunder	clamber	Esther
	molar	warship	boarder	clatter	ether
afterward	nectar		bother	cleaner	ever
altar	niggard	*er = ər*	bowler	clearer	faker
awkward	onward		broiler	cleaver	farmer
beggar	orchard	adder	broker	clever	farther
billiard	Oscar	after	brother	clincher	fisher
blizzard	pedlar	alter	bubbler	cluster	filler
briar	popular	amber	buffer	clutter	filter
bulwark	scholar	badger	butler	cobbler	finder
buzzard	solar	bailer	butter	copper	finger
burglar	steward	baker	camper	corner	flatter
Caesar	southward	banker	cancer	cover	flicker
cellar	Spaniard	banner	canter	cracker	flier
collar	standard	banter	censer	creamer	flitter
dollar	upwards	barber	center	desert	floater
forward	wayward	barter	chamber	differ	fluster
friar	westward	batter	chapter	digger	flutter
gizzard		beaker	charger	diner	flyer
grammar	*ar = or*	bearer	charter	dimmer	fodder
hangar		beaver	chatter	dinner	folder
Howard	award	better	checker	dipper	freezer
inward	lukewarm	bigger	chipper	dodger	freighter
inwards	quarrel	bitter	chopper	doer	further
laggard	quarter	bladder	cider	dresser	fuller
leopard	quartet	blister	cinder	ember	gambler
liar	quartzite	blotter	cistern	enter	gander
	reward				

gender	juggler	miner	pervade	Quaker	*or = ər*
ginger	jumper	mister	pervert	quitter	
giver	kaiser	monster	pester	raider	actor
glimmer	keeper	mower	picker	rancher	color
glitter	killer	neither	pilfer	rather	camphor
gobbler	lacquer	nether	planner	rattler	candor
gopher	ladder	number	planter	render	factor
govern	lantern	order	plaster	rider	humor
gunner	lather	pamper	platter	roadster	labor
gutter	laughter	panther	player	roaster	major
hammer	lawyer	paper	plier	robber	pallor
hamper	layer	partner	plotter	rocker	razor
hanger	leather	passer	plunder	roster	sailor
heater	lectern	patter	plunger	rover	tailor
herself	lower	pattern	poker	rubber	vapor
Homer	maker	peeler	ponder	rudder	valor
Hubert	manger	pepper	popper	runner	vector
hunter	marker	perhaps	primer	saber	
hurdler	master	permit	proper	setter	*yr = ər*
infer	matter	persist	prosper	settler	
jester	member	perspire	putter	signer	martyr
jigger	miller	persuade			zephyr

V

PUBLISHERS

Allyn and Bacon, Inc., Rockleigh, New Jersey 07647.

American Guidance Service, Inc., Circle Pines, Minnesota 55014.

Americana Interstate Corporation, Mundelein, Illinois 60060.

Ann Arbor Publishers, 611 Church, Ann Arbor, Michigan 48104.

Beckley-Cardy Company, 1900 N. Narragansett, Chicago, Illinois 60600.

Behavior Research Laboratories, Box 577, Palo Alto, California 94302.

Benefic Press, 10318 West Roosevelt Road, Westchester, Illinois 60153.

Benton Review Publishing Company, Inc., Fowler, Indiana 47944.

Brenner-Davis Phonics. Inc., 161 Green Bay Road, Wilmette, Illinois 60091.

Bureau of Publications, Teachers College, Columbia University, 525 West 120 Street, New York, New York 10027.

Chandler Publishing Company, 124 Spear Street, San Francisco, California, 94105.

Chester Electronic Laboratories, Chester, Connecticut 06412.

The Continental Press, Inc., Elizabethtown, Pennsylvania 17022.

Coronet Films, Inc., 65 East South Water Street, Chicago, Illinois 60601.

Craig Corporation, 3410 South LaCienega Boulevard, Los Angeles, California 90016.

Economy Company, 1901 North Walnut, Oklahoma City, Oklahoma 73125.

Educational Developmental Laboratories, Huntington, New York 11743.

Education Press, Visual Products Division 3M Company, Box 3344, St. Paul, Minnesota 55101.

Educational Publishing Corporation, Darien, Connecticut 06820.

Educators Publishing Service, Cambridge, Massachusetts 02139.

Educational Record Sales, 157 Chambers Street, New York, New York 10007.

Educational Service, Inc., P. O. Box 112, Benton Harbor, Michigan 49022.

Education Services Press, 3M Company, Box 3100, St. Paul, Minnesota 55100.

Expression Company, P. O. Box 11, Magnolia, Massachusetts 09130.

Eye Gate House, Inc., 146-01 Archer Avenue, Jamaica, New York 11400.

Feardon Publishers, 2165 Park Blvd., Palo Alto, California 94306.

Follett Publishing Company, 1010 West Washington Boulevard, Chicago, Illinois 60607.

Ginn and Company, 125 Second Avenue, Boston, Mass. 02154.

Harcourt, Brace and World, Inc., 757 Third Avenue, New York, New York 10017.

Holt, Rinehart and Winston, Inc., 383 Madison Avenue, New York, New York 10017.

Hoover Brothers, Kansas City, Missouri 64100.

174

Houghton Mifflin Company, 1900 South Batavia Avenue, Geneva, Illinois 60134.

Imperial Products, Inc., Kankakee, Illinois 60901.

Initial Teaching Alphabet Publications, Inc., 20 East 46th Street, New York, New York 10017.

Institute of Educational Research, Inc., Washington, D.C. 20000.

Kenworthy Educational Service, Inc., P.O. Box 3031, Buffalo, New York 14205.

Learning Materials, Inc., 100 East Ohio Street, Chicago, Illinois 60600.

Learning through Seeing, Inc., P.O. Box 368, Sunland, California 91040.

J. B. Lippincott Company, East Washington Square, Philadelphia, Pennsylvania, 19105.

Lyons and Carnahan, 407 East 25th St., Chicago, Illinois 60616.

The Macmillan Company, 866 Third Avenue, New York, New York, 10022.

McCormick Mathers Publishing Company, Inc., 1440 East English Street, Wichita, Kansas 67200.

McGraw-Hill Book Company, Inc., 330 West 42nd St. New York, New York 10036.

Charles E. Merrill Books, Inc., 1300 Alum Creek Drive, Columbus, Ohio 43216.

Modern Curriculum Press, P.O. Box 9, Berea, Ohio 44017.

O'Connor Reading Clinic Publishing Company, 1040 E. Maple Road, Birmingham, Michigan 48011.

F. A. Owen Publishing Company, Dansville, New York, 14437.

Pacific Productions, 2614 Etna Street, Berkeley, California 94700.

Phonovisual Products, Inc., 4708 Wisconsin Avenue, N.W., Washington, D.C. 20016.

Programmed Records, Inc., 154 Nassau Street, New York, New York 10000.

Science Research Associates, Inc., 259 East Erie Street, Chicago, Illinois, 60611.

Scott, Foresman and Company, 1900 East Lake Avenue, Glenview, Illinois, 60025.

L. W. Singer and Company, (a division of Random House, 249–259 West Erie Boulevard, Syracuse, New York 13200.

Society for Visual Education, Inc., (Subsidy of General Precision Equipment Corporation, Chicago, Illinois 60600).

The Steck-Vaughn Company, P.O. Box 2028, Austin, Texas 78767.

Systems for Education, Inc., 612 North Michigan Avenue, Chicago, Illinois 60611.

Webster Publishing Company, a division of McGraw-Hill Book Co., Manchester Road, Manchester, Missouri 63011.

Whiteside, Inc., 788 Bloomfield Avenue, Clifton, New Jersey 07012.

Whitman Publishing Company, 1220 Mound Avenue, Racine, Wisconsin 53404.

Wilcox and Follett, 1000 West Washington Boulevard, Chicago, Illinois 60600.

Wordcrafters Guild, St. Albans School, Washington, D.C. 20000.

REFERENCES

1. Aaron, I. E.: What teachers and prospective teachers know about phonic generalizations. *J Educ Res*, *53*:323–330, 1960.
2. Austin, M. C.: Kenney, H. J.: Gutman, A. R., and Fraggos, M.: *The Torch Lighters: Tommorrow's Teachers of Reading*. Cambridge, Harvard, 1961.
3. Bailey, M. H.: The utility of phonic generalization in grades one through six. *Reading Teacher*, *20*:413–418, 1967.
4. Barrett, T. C.: Performance on selected prereading tasks and first grade reading achievement. In *Vistas in Reading*. New York, Int. Read. Ass., 1967, pp. 461–464.
5. Barrett, T. C.: Visual discrimination tasks as predictors of first grade reading achievement. *Reading Teacher*, *18:* 276–282, 1965.
6. Berry, M. F., and Eisenson, J.: *Speech Disorders: Principles and Practice of Therapy*. New York, Appleton, 1956.
7. Betts, E. A.: Issues in teaching reading. In *Controversial Issues in Reading*. Tenth Annual Reading Conference, Lehigh University, 1961, pp. 33–41.
8. Bloomfield, L.: Linguistics and reading. *Elementary English*, *19*:125–130, 183–186, 1942.
9. Bloomfield, L., and Barnhart, C. L.: *Let's Read: A Linguistic Approach*. Detroit, Wayne, 1961.
10. Botel, M.: Strategies for teaching sound-letter relationships. In *Vistas in Reading*. New York, Int. Read. Ass., 1967, pp. 156–159.
11. Bugelski, B. R.: *The Psychology of Learning Applied to Teaching*. Indianapolis, Bobbs, 1964.
12. Burmeister, L. E.: Usefulness of phonic generalizations. *Reading Teacher*, *21*:349–356, 360, 1968.
13. Burmeister, L. E.: Vowel pairs. *Reading Teacher*, *21*:445–452, 1968.
14. Cole, L.: *The Improvement of Reading with Special Reference to Remedial Instruction*. New York, Holt, 1938.
15. Coleman, E. B.: Experimental studies of readability, *Elementary English*, *45*:166–178, 1968.
16. Connell, D.: Auditory and visual discrimination in kindergarten. *Elementary English*, *45*:51–54, 66, 1968.
17. Davis, I. P.: The speech aspects of reading readiness. *National Elementary Principal*, *17:*282–288, 1938.
18. DeBoer, J. J., and Dallman, M.: *The Teaching of Reading*. New York, Holt, 1960, p. 105.
19. Dechant, E.: *Improving the Teaching of Reading*. Englewood Cliffs, N. J., Prentice-Hall, 1964.

20. Durrell, D. D.: First-grade reading success study: a summary. *J Educ, 140*:2–6, 1958.

21. Durrell, D. D., and Murphy, H. A.: The auditory discrimination factor in reading readiness and reading disability. *Education, 73*:556–560, 1953.

22. Durrell, D. D., and Nicholson, A. K.: Preschool and kindergarten experience. In *Development in and Through Reading*, Sixtieth Yearbook, N.S.S.E., Chicago, U. of Chicago, 1961, pp. 257–269.

23. Edwards, T. J.: Teaching reading: a critique. In Money, J. (Ed.): *The Disabled Reader*. Baltimore, Johns Hopkins, 1966, pp. 349–362.

24. Emans, R.: When two vowels go walking and other such things. *Reading Teacher, 21*:262–269, 1967.

25. Fries, C. C.: *Linguistics and Reading*. New York, Holt, 1963.

26. Fry, E.: A frequency approach to phonics. *Elementary English, 51*:759–765, 1964.

27. Glass, G. G.: The strange world of syllabication. *Elementary School Journal*, 403–405, 1967.

28. Hanna, R. R., and Moore, T. Jr.: Spelling—From spoken word to written symbol. *Elementary School J, 53:* 329–337, 1953.

29. Hanson, I. W.: First grade children work with variant word endings. *Reading Teacher, 19*:505–507, 511, 1966.

30. Harris, A. J.: *How to Increase Reading Ability*. New York, McKay, 1956.

31. Herr, S. E.: *Learning Activities for Reading*. Dubuque, Brown, W. C., 1961, p. 88.

32. Hildreth, G.: *Teaching Reading*. New York, Holt, 1958.

33. Hockett, C. F.: *A Course in Modern Linguistics*. New York, Macmillan, 1958, p. 24.

34. Joos, L. W.: Linguistics for the dyslexic. In Money, J. (Ed.): *The Disabled Reader*. Baltimore, Johns Hopkins, 1966, pp. 83–92.

35. Keislar, E.: Conference on perceptual and linguistic aspects of reading. *Reading Teacher, 18*:43–49, 1964.

36. Lefevre, C. A.: *Linguistics and the Teaching of Reading*. New York, McGraw, 1964.

37. Lefevre, C. A.: Reading our language patterns: a linguistic view—contributions to a theory of reading. *Challenge and Experiment in Reading, International Reading Association Conference, 7*:66–70, 1962.

38. Levin, H.: Reading research: what, why, and for whom. *Elementary English, 43*:138–147, 1966.

39. Levin, H., and Watson, J.: The learning of variable grapheme-to-phoneme correspondences. In Levin, H., *et al.: A Basic Research Program on Reading*, final report, Coop Res Project No. 639.

40. McKee, P.: *Reading: A Program for the Elementary School*. Boston, Houghton, 1966, p. 74.

41. Morency, A. S.; Wepman, J. M., and Weiner, P. S.: Studies in speech: developmental articulation inaccuracy. *Elementary School J, 67*:329–337, 1967.

42. Newburg, J. E.: *Linguistics and the School Curriculum*. Chicago, Sci. Res. Assoc.

43. Orton, S. T.: An impediment to learning to read—a neurological explanation of the reading disability. *School and Society, 28*:286–290, 1928.

44. Platts, M. E.; Sister Rose Marguerite, and Shumaker, E.: *Spice*. Washington, Educational Services, p. 143.
45. Poole, I.: Genetic Development of articulation of consonant sounds in speech. *Elementary Eng Rev, 11:*159–161, 1934.
46. Popp, H. M.: Visual discrimination of alphabet letters. *Reading Teacher, 17:*221–225, 1964.
47. Ramsey, Z. W.: Will tomorrow's teachers know and teach phonics? *Reading Teacher, 15:*241–245, 1962.
48. Sabaroff, R.: Breaking the code: what method? Introducing an integrated linguistic approach to beginning reading. *Elementary School J, 67:*95–102, 1966.
49. Schnell, L. M.: Teaching structural analysis. *Reading Teacher, 21:*133–137, 1967.
50. Spache, G. D., and Baggett, M. E.: What do teachers know about phonics and syllabication? *Reading Teacher, 19:*96–99, 1965.
51. Van Riper, C., and Butler, K. G.: *Speech in the Elementary Classroom*. New York, Harper, 1955.
52. Weber, R.: "A Linguistic Analysis of First Grade Reading Errors." 1966 mimeo. In William, J. P., and Levin, H.: Word perception: psychological bases. *Education, 87:*515–518, 1967.
53. Wheelock, W. H., and Silvaroli, N. J.: Visual discrimination training for beginning readers. *Reading Teacher, 21:*115–120, 1967.

INDEX